WHAT'S
GOD GOT TO DO WITH THE
AMERICAN EXPERIMENT?

WHAT'S GOD GOT TO DO WITH THE AMERICAN EXPERIMENT?

E.J. DIONNE JR.
JOHN J. DIIULIO JR.

Editors

BROOKINGS INSTITUTION PRESS
Washington, D.C.

About Brookings

The Brookings Institution is a private nonprofit organization devoted to research, education, and publication on important issues of domestic and foreign policy. Its principal purpose is to bring knowledge to bear on current and emerging policy problems. The Institution maintains a position of neutrality on issues of public policy. Interpretations or conclusions in Brookings publications should be understood to be solely those of the authors.

Copyright © 2000 by

THE BROOKINGS INSTITUTION

1775 Massachusetts Avenue, N.W., Washington, D.C. 20036

Taylor Branch's chapter is reprinted with the permission of
Simon & Schuster from *Parting the Waters* by Taylor Branch.
Copyright © 1988 by Taylor Branch.

Library of Congress Cataloging-in-Publication data

What's God got to do with the American experiment? /
  E.J. Dionne Jr. and John J. DiIulio Jr., editors.
    p.   cm.
Includes bibliographical references and index.
  ISBN 0-8157-1869-1 (alk. paper)
    1. United States—Religion—1960– 2. Religion and politics—United
States. 3. Christianity and politics—United States. I. Dionne, E. J.
II. DiIulio, John J.
  BL2525 .W47 2000   00-009635
  200'.973'09045—dc21   CIP

              9 8 7 6 5 4 3 2 1

The paper used in this publication meets the minimum requirements of the
American National Standard for Information Sciences—Permanence
of Paper for Printed Library Materials: ANSI Z39.48-1984.

Typeset in Adobe Garamond

Composition by Cynthia Stock
Silver Spring, Maryland

Printed by R. R. Donnelley & Sons Co.
Harrisonburg, Virginia

For
Mary, James, Julia, and Margot
Rosalee, Elizabeth, John Peter, and Daniel

Contents

Foreword

GLENN   LOURY

As a social scientist I now find it imperative to think seriously about the "God talk" we hear with increasing frequency these days and to consider what it might mean for formulating and executing public policy. In recent years I have grown dissatisfied with the clinical, abstract accounts of human behavior that underlie our purportedly scientific study of society. The human beings in these accounts are soulless creatures—utility-maximizing buyers and sellers, behaviorally conditioned violators of the law, genetically predisposed substance abusers, and the like. This brand of social science propounds theories about the mechanisms of human action that omit any consideration of what most makes us human—our awareness of our own mortality and our fitful, uncertain, often unsuccessful attempts to give our lives some meaning that just might transcend our pitifully brief existence. My sense is that this omission has left social scientists less well equipped to prescribe remedies for the most serious social problems that our societies now confront.

Permit me to offer an illustration. One of the leading social scientists of our time is James Q. Wilson, whose article in this book is worthy of particularly close attention. Over the years Wilson has written wisely and well about how parents discipline their children and about the consequences of such behavior for the later-life sociability of their charges. He has argued that regularly providing modest positive and negative reinforcements to a young child for good and bad actions lowers the risk of antisocial behavior as the child enters adolescence. Once allowed to develop, these antisocial behaviors are hard to change. So if the character-shaping tutelage of vigilant parents is missing in early childhood, the young adult who emerges may turn out to be incorrigible.

This is a matter of no small policy significance, since millions of children in the most disadvantaged quarters of our society are growing to maturity absent conscientiously applied parental discipline. And yet, a great many people connected with religious institutions are laboring, in the most marginal of American communities, to turn these "incorrigibles" in a different direction. These religiously inspired activists confront young adults who received neither proper nutrition in infancy nor sufficient verbal stimulation as toddlers, who never learned to internalize as second nature the difference between right and wrong, and who have committed the acts that incorrigible, undisciplined adolescents commit. Yet despite all that, with God's help, as they would say, these lives have been turned around.

What is interesting to me—as a social scientist, to be sure, but also as a citizen—is what I will call the antideterministic character in this way of thinking. Most social science offers deterministic accounts of human action, with some probability distribution around the predicted behavior that is meant to account for errors in our observations. Our theories say, in effect, that material conditions mediated by social institutions cause us to behave in a certain way. Yet surely it is more plausible to hold that material and institutional givens can at best establish only a fairly wide range within which behavior must lie, and that the specific actions within this range for any particular human being will depend on motivation, will, and spirit— that is, on what a person takes to be the source of meaning in his or her life, on what animates him or her at the deepest level.

If this is right, then what is crucial to grasp is the implication that the behavior of freely choosing, socially situated, spiritually endowed human beings will in some essential way be indeterminate, unpredictable, even mysterious. For if human behavior is in substantial part a consequence of what people understand to be meaningful, of what they believe in, then the processes of social interaction and mutual stimulation that generate and

sustain patterns of belief in human communities become centrally important. But these processes—persuasion, conformity, conversion, myth construction, and the like—are open ended. They are, at best, only weakly
constrained by material conditions. That is, while what we believe about
the transcendent powerfully shapes how we act in a given situation, these
beliefs cannot themselves be deduced as a necessary consequence of our
situation. We can always agree to believe differently, or more fervently—
particularly if those with whom we are most closely connected are under-
going a similar transformation. Religious revivals and reformations can
sweep through our ranks and change our collective view of the world virtually overnight. We can be moved to make enormous sacrifices on behalf of
abstract goals. We are ever capable, as Vaclav Havel has said so well, of
"transcending the world of existences."

I admit to being deeply moved by this fact about human experience—
that we are spiritual creatures, generators of meaning, beings that must not
and cannot "live by bread alone." I have seen the power for good (and for
ill) of communal organization acting through the constitution of collectivities that are like-minded in their understandings about the meaning of
life, about, as the believers say, "what God put us here for."

Until social science takes this aspect of the human drama with the
utmost seriousness, it will do justice neither to its subjects of study nor to
the national community that looks to it for useful advice about a host of
social ills.

An important consideration here, of course, is the proper role of government. I would like to conclude with this observation: however one reads
the Constitution, the fact is that, willy-nilly, government must play an
important role in that process of belief construction and propagation. We
are not going to withdraw from the public support of indigent families or
public provision of educational services, or from the maintenance of civil
order through the coercive institutions of policing and incarceration. Bil-
lions of public dollars will be spent, and public institutions are going to be
created. This money and these institutions will interact, helpfully or not,
with what communities of believers are trying to achieve. The centrality of
religious experience in the lives of so many Americans must therefore be
reckoned with by the prudent exponent of public policy.

For my own part, I pray that broadly based, deeply rooted, powerfully led, spiritually anointed movements in our most disadvantaged communities will not just be tolerated by our public institutions, but that as a nation we will find ways of supporting these communities of faith as they seek—in mysterious and unpredictable ways—to transform, and to transcend, the social reality.

Acknowledgments

THIS COLLECTION has been a joy to produce because the authors whose work is included have been a joy to work with. We begin by thanking them for allowing us to include their writing in this volume. It is ecumenical in both religious and political terms. We hope the coexistence of all these authors under one virtual roof might suggest that dialogue and disagreement on one of the most sensitive issues in public life can be fruitful, civil, and even, sometimes, good humored.

The book would not exist without the exceptional work of Staci Simmons and Brenda Szittya. Staci has been at the center of much of the Brookings Institution's recent work on religion and public life, and she made sure this book happened. She is a diplomat, a brilliant organizer, a warm-hearted taskmaster, an insightful thinker, and a reflective person of faith. Some say kindness and efficacy don't go together. They've not met Staci.

As editor of the *Brookings Review*, Brenda encouraged us to guest edit the Spring 1999 issue of the magazine, which provided the first home for many of these essays. She helped us again when we substantially expanded the number of essays and the reach of topics. Brenda is a gifted editor because she loves not only words but also those who work with them. She got the most out of all of us—and made it easy for all of us to enjoy it. Thanks to Mary Boyle for inspiring the title and for much more. And thanks to Mike Cromartie, Keith Pavlischek, and our three Civitas fellows: Timothy Shah, W. Bradford Wilcox, and Ruth Melkonian-Hoover.

As we explain in the introduction, this project had its origins in con-ferences organized in 1997 around Ram Cnaan's work with Partners for Sacred Places. Those meetings could not have been organized without the superb work of Kristen Lippert-Martin and Cindy Brodbeck, who also gave critical help in the creation of this book. And neither the meetings nor the book would have happened without the support of the Pew Charitable Trusts and the director of their religion program, Luis Lugo. Luis's civic-minded approach to the subject has not only given birth to important new research (a bit of it captured here) but also inspired new hope that diverse communities can give life to new partnerships—among religious groups, between religious and secular groups, and between the private and public spheres—to enhance the life prospects of our neediest neighbors. Ye shall know them by their works, and the new works by the Trusts on behalf of poor urban children, youth, and families shall be known as good.

Perhaps 200 people were involved in those 1997 meetings, and we cannot thank them all here. But particular thanks go to Ram Cnaan, James Q. Wilson, William Bennett, Senator Joseph Lieberman, the Reverend Eugene Rivers, Glenn Loury, the Reverend James P. Wind, Kent Greenawalt, and Pam Solo for playing central roles. As representative of those who en-livened our meetings, we list just a few of the participants: the Reverend Susan Johnson, Father Michael Doyle, the Reverend Cheryl Sanders, Julie Siegel, Sharon Parrott, and Steve Berger.

At Brookings, we have received exceptional support. Brookings Presi-dent Michael Armacost has been consistently and thoughtfully encourag-ing of our explorations in religion and public life. At an institution that has dedicated itself to detailed policy research in economics, foreign policy, politics, and government reform, Mike saw how important religion and those inspired by faith can be in all these spheres. Paul Light, director of the Governmental Studies program, has been a dynamo. He thinks as fast as he talks and writes as fast as he thinks. That he has many good ideas is well known to all who have read his work. That he puts many of his best ideas (and so much of his energy) to the service of his colleagues should also be known. And there is no way to give adequate thanks to our delight-ful friend and loyal Brookings colleague Tom Mann. Our other colleagues in the Governmental Studies program are a blessing and inspiring examples.

The Brookings Press has been enthusiastic from beginning to end. Bob Faherty, director of the press, brought to this book not only the skills of one of the most energetic publishers around but also a personal commitment to and interest in the subject. We are grateful. Susan Woollen has a great gift for design and a love of her work, which she shares with everyone. Theresa Walker is thoughtful, meticulous, and understanding—just the gifts you need in a copy editor.

For permission to reprint, expand upon, or revise pieces that were published earlier, we thank the *American Prospect,* the *Washington Post,* the *Responsive Community,* Simon and Schuster, the Van Andel Education Institute, and the J. M. Dawson Institute of Church-State Studies.

Although this is a book about faith and its impact on public life, and although some of our contributors are preachers by trade, we hope it reflects the passion of our authors without being too preachy. But these two Catholics would not be honest if we didn't acknowledge that our commitment to the subject at hand is also personal. We try to pay heed to the letter of James and his insistence that faith without works is dead. We thus close by thanking those in the churches, synagogues, mosques, and elsewhere who give of themselves to help their fellow citizens, strengthen their communities, and make America a nation that loves and honors the sick and the dying, the poor, and the oppressed. May their work be appreciated and blessed.

EJD
JJD

WHAT'S GOD GOT TO DO WITH THE AMERICAN EXPERIMENT?

1

God and the American Experiment

An Introduction

E. J. DIONNE JR. AND
JOHN J. DIIULIO JR.

ONE COULD IMAGINE the question posed in the title of this book provoking two legions to mass against each other. They'd offer sharply different accounts of the role of God and organized religion in creating and nurturing the American experiment.

In one view, it is America's pluralistic and secular Constitution that has promoted freedom, diversity, and, oddly, the very strength of American religious communities. A state independent of organized religion has been freedom's, and religion's, finest friend. Was not a central motivation for the creation of free and tolerant institutions a desire to end wars over God and religion?

In the other account, freedom itself is rooted in a theistic—many would say Judeo-Christian—commitment to the inviolable dignity of the individual human being. This belief arises, in the words of the Declaration of Independence, from "the Law of Nature and of Nature's God." A belief in God places healthy restraints on the human tendency to deify political systems or individual political strongmen—and insists that even strongmen are accountable to a Higher Authority.

This argument is as old as our republic, and in truth the two views just offered are not mutually exclusive. The essays presented in this book make no pretense of settling the debate definitively. As Alan Wolfe writes in these pages, "Two hundred years after the brilliant writings of James Madison and Thomas Jefferson on the topic, Americans cannot make up their minds whether religion is primarily private, public, or some uneasy combination of the two." But precisely because of the ambiguities Wolfe describes, arguments about the role of God and religious faith in our democracy are now, and always have been, central to our understanding of its workings.

Wolfe's comments remind us why we should not be surprised that religion and questions surrounding it played such a large role in the early rounds of the 2000 presidential campaign. While it could not be predicted that Governor George W. Bush would say in a debate that Jesus Christ was his favorite political philosopher, one could predict that Bush's answer—and his explanation for it—would arouse intense debate. When asked to explain why he had named Jesus and how Jesus had changed his life, Bush replied, "Well, if they don't know, it's going to be hard to explain."

Many evangelical Christians knew exactly how Bush felt and identified with his answer. Not surprisingly, conservative Evangelicals became his most loyal supporters in his intense primary battle with Senator John McCain. Yet many Catholics and Jews, mainline Protestants, and nonbelievers saw Bush's answer as inadequate or worse. "In principle, it's appropriate for a religious candidate to make known and explain his religious convictions. It leads to a richer and more informed public debate," said Father J. Bryan Hehir, a professor at Harvard Divinity School. But Father Hehir added, "Religion is certainly about the heart, but it's about more than the heart. It's about an intellectual structure of belief, and a candidate needs to explain what that intellectual structure is about. And that was totally missing from Bush's answer."

That was only the first skirmish. Bush's visit to Bob Jones University unleashed attacks from Democrats but also from McCain who pointed to the school's history of racism and anti-Catholicism. Bush captured the conservative evangelical vote and won the crucial South Carolina primary. But McCain capitalized on a backlash to the Bush tactics by, among things, launching thousands of phone calls to Catholic voters in Michigan, where the subsequent primary was held, informing them of Bush's Bob Jones visit and the university's attitude toward Catholics. McCain then raised the stakes around the religious issue by denouncing Christian conservative leaders, the Reverends Pat Robertson and Jerry Falwell, both of them Bush supporters. All this happened within just the first few months of Campaign 2000.

When religious issues of this sort arise in political campaigns, the response is usually rapid polarization around absolute positions held with utter conviction. Yet absolute answers to questions about the relationship of religious faith to our democratic life tend to obscure as much as they illuminate. The history of religion's relationship to America's democratic freedoms is told quite differently within different faiths, denominations, and political communities.

We Americans—almost all of us—can be quite inconsistent in our views of how and when religion should influence politics. Many who welcome the prophetic role of the churches in movements to abolish slavery, promote civil rights, and secure social justice are skeptical of applying religion's prophetic voice to matters such as abortion, sexuality, or family life. Many who welcome the second set of commitments can be just as wary of crusades rooted in a social gospel. Richard Parker's essay is an important reminder that for all the emphasis in standard contemporary accounts about the role of the religious right, some of the most compelling action on the progressive side of politics is being organized through religious institutions. Citing a Methodist document on the economy, Parker notes that "the Methodists' vision is much more progressive than anything emanating from Democratic Party platforms or policies in the last thirty years." In another powerful challenge to our stereotypes about the relationship between religious faith and action, W. Bradford Wilcox and John P. Bartkowski argue that the evidence shows conservative Protestants to have an approach to family life "in many ways more progressive" than that of other Americans.

In his autobiography, *Strength for the Journey*, the Reverend Jerry Falwell is admirably candid in acknowledging the contrast between his reaction to church-based civil rights activists in 1965 ("Preachers are not called upon to be politicians but to be soul winners," he said then) and his later embrace of political activism in response to the Supreme Court's 1973 decision legalizing abortion. Falwell's words are worth remembering as you read Taylor Branch's powerful essay—drawn from his book *Parting the Waters*—on Martin Luther King's address on the Montgomery bus boycott. To contrast King with Falwell, or Falwell's earlier views with his later views, is to learn a healthy wariness about sweeping statements concerning the relationship between religion and public life.

God Meets the Social Scientist

While there is a long and honorable history of engagement between social science and the study of religion (from Max Weber and Emile Durkheim to Will Herberg, Robert Bellah, and Andrew Greeley), arguments about God and politics rarely stay on the neutral ground defined by the statistical techniques that give comfort to social scientists. For believers, the final answers can never lie in factor analysis or regression coefficients.

Yet paradoxically, the origins of this book lie precisely in that old tradition of social science research. An organization dedicated to saving historic church buildings, Partners for Sacred Places, invited Ram Cnaan of the University of Pennsylvania to conduct a classic form of the social science study. Partners wanted to know what inner-city congregations were doing to meet the social needs of their neighborhoods. What kind of services did they provide and to whom?

Cnaan did what social scientists do: he conducted a survey, in his case of 113 congregations in Chicago, Indianapolis, Mobile, New York, Philadelphia, and San Francisco. The results of Cnaan's work, reported in these pages, were unsurprising to those who knew what was happening in the religious institutions and yet dramatic nonetheless. Reacting to this study, William J. Bennett noted that social science often involves "the elaborate demonstration of the obvious by methods that are obscure." Cnann used the most staightforward methodology to capture what people in the trenches of community work see every day.

Simply put: the congregations do a great deal. They set up soup kitchens and feeding programs for the homeless, recreational programs for young children and teens, alliances with neighborhood associations, clothing drives, and important forms of fellowship for the elderly and the sick. One of

Cnaan's most important findings is that congregation members performed these services not primarily on behalf of one another but for those outside their ranks. This was, to use a favorite term of both social scientists and theologians, "other-regarding" work.

Sacred Places, Civic Purposes

Cnaan's findings are consistent with those of other social scientists. Father Andrew Greeley aptly summarized the evidence in an essay in the *American Prospect*. The research has consistently shown that both "frequency of church attendance and membership in church organizations correlate strongly with voluntary service."[1] The best available data suggest that religious organizations and "relationships related to religion" are clearly the major forces mobilizing volunteers in America. Even a third of secular volunteers— people who did not volunteer for specifically religious activities—relate their service "to the influence of a relationship based on their religion." Sacred places, it seems, serve civic purposes.

What grew out of the Cnaan study, thanks to help from the Pew Charitable Trusts and the energetic work of Luis Lugo, the director of its religion program, were two meetings sponsored by Brookings in 1997. At the first, in November, Cnaan presented his findings for comment from Senator Joseph Lieberman, William Bennett, and a group of inner-city pastors.

At the second meeting, in December, a broad group of activists, religious leaders, and social scientists debated the role of religiously based institutions in alleviating poverty. They addressed in particular the proper relationship of government to this work.

The ensuing debate was lively and moving, and it crossed many political lines. At times, representatives of the Gospel Mission movement seemed to share common ground with a representative of Americans United for the Separation of Church and State. Liberals and conservatives, often at odds on many questions, shared a hopefulness about the activities of churches as providers of services to the poor, as prophetic voices on their behalf, and, in the words of Father Michael Doyle of Sacred Heart Church in Camden, N.J., as "base operators of great community organizing, where people can be brought together to do for themselves." It's fair to say that the spirit of the meeting was captured in an adage coined by Martin Luther King. In the struggle against injustice, King said, "God isn't going to do all of it by Himself."

This book grows out of those meetings. Some of the essays (by Ram Cnaan, Glenn Loury, James Q. Wilson, and John DiIulio) are revised and, especially in Wilson's case, extended versions of their remarks and papers. We have added many new essays, including reports to provide a baseline for the debate—Richard N. Ostling's historical look at the changes in the nation's religious landscape and an examination of public attitudes by Robert Blendon, Richard Morin, and their colleagues.

A "Passion for the Possible"

The interest in faith-based charity should be seen as a particularly promising aspect of a larger transformation in the discussion of religion and politics in America. To characterize the new discussion in what some might see as an excessively optimistic light, it does appear (despite the polarized politics of the 2000 Republican primaries) that many among devout believers are more sensitive than their forebears might have been to the demands of religious pluralism and tolerance; and that many Americans inclined toward secularism are more alive now than they were even a decade ago to the contributions made by religious people and institutions to social renewal. "The role of government at all levels is being redefined, but so is the role of religion," Jim Wind of the Alban Institute said at the December meeting. "We must find new ways to think about the relationship of religion and public life."

There is also an opening toward a more nuanced understanding of the interaction between religious commitment and social change, between personal transformation and social justice. That both Bush and Vice President Al Gore have endorsed government help to "faith-based organizations" suggests how much the debate had changed and reflects a new recognition of the power of these institutions to solve problems. And, as evangelical writer and activist Jim Wallis points out in his essay, these institutions are now so much part of the public policy debate that they have their own wonky set of initials. They are now known as "FBOs." The importance of these groups is futher underscored in the essays by two former mayors, Stephen Goldmith, a Republican from Indianapolis who is a leading policy adviser to Governor Bush's campaign, and Kurt Schmoke, a Democrat from Baltimore.

Yet even the strongest advocates of the FBOs ackowledge that religion's role in renewing society will most often begin at the level of the individual, not the government. "Religion's chief contribution to morality is to enable people to transform their lives," Wilson writes. "Faith can only transform one person at a time, and then only as the result of the personal attention of one other person."

Patrick Glynn makes a powerful parallel case. "Religion does its real work in politics not by arousing moral indignation, but by awakening the individual conscience," he writes. "The distinction is a subtle but important one. Moral indignation drives us to condemn others; conscience prompts us to question ourselves." Or, as the theologian Jurgen Moltmann said of Christian hope, "It will constantly arouse the 'passion for the possible,' inventiveness and elasticity in self-transformation, in breaking with the old and coming to terms with the new."

Contemporary talk about "opportunity" and "responsibility" among both Democratic and Republican politicians reflects another aspect of this search for balance. As Glenn Loury put it in an essay in the *New York Times* discussing conservatism, a mature public philosophy "acknowledges personal responsibility as one part of the social contract, but also understands the importance of collective responsibility."[2] In Glynn's terms, conscience may prompt individuals to change their own behavior and also prompt them to become agents of social change. The role of faith in either case is not to impose itself through the state but to move individual citizens to demand greater responsibility from themselves and from their institutions.

There is also this overarching fact: all the reports of the death of organized religion and religious sentiment in America have been greatly exaggerated. Since the end of World War II, we have witnessed what Roger Finke and Rodney Stark have aptly described as the "churching of America," resulting by the mid-1990s in a nation with an estimated half-million churches, synagogues, and mosques, 2,000 or more religious denominations, and an unknown number of independent churches. In 1995 Gallup's Religion Index, an ongoing measurement of the religious beliefs and practices of the American public, hit a ten-year high. That same year, Nobel economist Robert W. Fogel of the University of Chicago speculated that the United States was in the midst of "its Fourth Great Awakening," a "new religious revival." Staci Simmons's comment on the WWJD?—What Would Jesus Do?—phenomenon is a further piece of evidence for Fogel's assertion.

Charitable Choice

Great Awakening or not, public laws have grown more "faith friendly." The federal government's latest welfare overhaul (a bill, it might be noted, criticized by both authors of this essay in many of its other aspects) includes what was labeled the Charitable Choice provision. It encourages states to use "faith-based organizations in serving the poor and needy" and requires that religious organizations be permitted to receive contracts, vouchers, and other government funding on the same basis as any other nongovernmental providers of services. Importantly, the measure includes a provision designed to protect "the religious integrity and character of faith-based organizations that are willing to accept government funds."

As enacted in 1996, Charitable Choice covers each of the major federal antipoverty and social welfare programs (Temporary Assistance to Needy Families, Medicaid, Supplemental Security Income, and food stamps). Some are now proposing to expand Charitable Choice to juvenile justice programs and other federal policy domains. Many states, notably Texas, have moved aggressively to reorient their antipoverty programs around Charitable Choice.

Charitable Choice has largely been supported by conservatives and opposed by liberals—with some important exceptions such as Senator Paul Wellstone of Minnesota. But that is only part of the story, and Gore's endorsement of Charitable Choice suggests the story is still developing. A 1998 survey of 1,236 religious congregations by Mark Chaves of the University of Arizona found that the law may prove of far more benefit to the more liberal congregations. "Politically conservative congregations are much less likely to apply for government funds than are middle-of-the-road or liberal congregations," Chaves found. He also reported that predominantly African-American congregations are "very substantially more likely to be willing to apply for government funds than are white congregations."

In one sense, this is not surprising: more liberal congregations, and especially the African-American churches, have strong traditions of social outreach to the poor and, in many cases, a history of accepting federal funds in other spheres. Ronald J. Sider and Heidi Rolland Unruh cite one study's finding that 63 percent of faith-based child service agencies already receive a fifth or more of their budgets from public funds.

Still, these studies bring home the distortions that can be introduced into discussions of faith-based social services if they are seen only through the liberal-conservative lens. As Chaves notes, "If charitable choice initiatives are successful in reaching American congregations, the congregations most likely to take advantage of them may not be the ones our political and religious leaders expect to take advantage."[3] The more liberal churches may benefit from a conservative initiative.

While Sider and Unruh make a strong and, we think, quite convincing case for Charitable Choice, making Charitable Choice work remains an enormous challenge because constitutional worries about the free exercise of religion cannot be lightly dismissed.

Seen from the perspective of religious groups, there is the danger that entanglement with government will require them to weaken or water down their faith commitments, no matter how strongly the law tilts in their favor. Seen from the perspective of those fearful of intimate ties between government and religion, there is legitimate worry that supporting the religious groups with the highest success rates will entail government aid to precisely those organizations that require the strongest level of religious commitment from participants. As scholars such as Sider, Unruh, and Amy Sherman have found, the more spiritually demanding programs appear to produce the best results.[4] Those who fear that government support of religiously based charities could move quickly into "excessive entanglement" with religion can cite the most optimistic research on the success of such programs to justify their concerns. These fears are powerfully expressed in these pages by Melissa Rogers of the Baptist Joint Committee. She argues that too much government help to the good works carried out by religious congregations is "the wrong way to do right."

Wilson's suggestion that we "facilitate the movement of private funds into church-connected enterprises" could provide a useful tool for strengthening the work of the congregations while placing reasonable limitations on government involvement. The truth is that these organizations always will—and always should—rely primarily on private support. Finding a way to strengthen these institutions without implicating government too deeply in their work is the conundrum. One of the most heartening aspects of the current debate is a new openness across political lines to a search for balance that might resolve it.

Religious Wars

To be sure, the debates about religion and politics to which we have become accustomed since the late 1970s have not gone away. The mere mention of government-supported vouchers to allow children to go to religious schools can unleash a furious debate over the meaning of the First Amendment and whether or not it really requires a "wall of separation." Controversy over the role of the Christian Coalition and other groups of religious conservatives has sharpened in the early stages of the 2000 campaign. Even within religious conservative ranks, as the essay here by Cal Thomas and Ed Dobson shows, there is a great debate over whether religiously motivated political activists are being "seduced by the siren song of temporal political power," as Thomas and Dobson put it.

The battle over President Clinton's impeachment aggravated relations between liberals (both religious and secular) and organized religious conservatives. Attacks on the Christian right appeared quite effective for many Democratic candidates in the 1998 elections. The insistence by Christian conservative groups that Congress go ahead with impeaching the president in the face of the election results appeared to play a large role in getting impeachment articles through the House of Representatives to the Senate.

Several essays here explore the Clinton episode, which is destined for some time to shape—and perhaps distort—discussions of religion, morality, and politics. For all the honorable talk about putting the dreadful matter "behind us," a battle so divisive and so resonant with both moral and partisan meanings is certain to leave a long-lasting imprint on American political discourse.

Many combatants on both sides of the Clinton case were moved to seek religious justifications for their positions. In the final months of the controversy, there was a running argument among pro- and anti-Clinton religious factions about the definitions of forgiveness, the requirements of repentance, and the public use of religious symbols.

There seemed to be a contest over which injunctions mattered most—Judge not lest ye be judged was stacked up against Thou shall not commit adultery or bear false witness. It was possible to harbor, of both sides, a suspicion that C. S. Lewis voiced decades ago about his fellow Christians: "Most of us are not really approaching the subject in order to find out what Christianity says. We are approaching it in the hope of finding support from Christianity for the views of our own party." Peter Wehner's essay, inspired by Lewis's *Screwtape Letters*, is an amusing but trenchant comment on the dangers of putting religion to the service of politics. Wehner, a conservative activist, offers a strong warning to his own side—but not just to his own side.

The religious confusion bred by the Clinton scandal debate inspired some 140 theologians to issue a "Declaration concerning Religion, Ethics, and the Crisis in the Clinton Presidency," later published with a volume of essays on the subject, *Judgment Day at the White House*.[5] It is discussed and critiqued here in a thoughtful essay by Alan Wolfe. Wolfe warns that "any attempt to judge political leaders by the standards of religious values raises questions about which values should be used." Wolfe shares the suspicions of the declaration's signers about the president's decision "to seek the judgment of God [and] his fellow parishioners in highly visible, seemingly orchestrated, ways." Yet he worries that "not only are they judging Mr. Clinton's actions, they are also judging the depths of his religious beliefs." This is an awkward issue to raise in a society that is characterized by religious pluralism—and that has long resisted religious tests for those in public office. But Jean Bethke Elshtain, one of the organizers of the declaration, offers a powerful defense of its premises, arguing that "one cannot drive a wedge between ethics and politics" and warning against what she calls "amoral Machiavellianism." The distinguished theologian Max Stackhouse also offers a brief reply to Wolfe's argument.

Few in America felt the awkwardness of the president's very public search for redemption more personally than the Reverend Tony Campolo, who became one of the president's spiritual counselors. His essay is a document of our time, a reflection on what it feels like to be caught in the crossfire of a religious skirmish in a political war. One might note this irony: those who criticized Campolo for putting religion to the service of politics may have been calling upon him to do precisely that—to resist the opportunity to minister to the president because of a widespread belief that the president's quest for counseling was Machiavellian, not authentically spiritual. That Campolo would not have run into such public resistance had he instead counseled a convicted murderer on death row raises interesting questions.

Religion-in-Public

Campolo's difficulties help explain why religion's relationship to public life is such a vexing issue. As a country, we are terribly torn about what religion-in-public should mean. Collectively, we seem suspicious of politicians who are too religious and suspicious of politicians who are not religious at all. This can lead to the very worst forms of religious expression. As Gregg Easterbrook writes in his recent book, *Beside Still Waters*: "If a politician or celebrity stands up to mumble about being blessed by the Lord, and speaks in a manner unmistakably vacuous and intended for public consumption, nobody minds. If the same person says with conviction, I really believe my faith requires me to do this or that, the expression will be condemned as inappropriate."[6]

The paradoxes of religious faith are obvious. It can create community, and it can divide communities. It can lead to searing self-criticism, and it can promote a pompous self-satisfaction. It can encourage dissent and conformity, generosity and narrow-mindedness. It can engender both righteous behavior and self-righteousness. Its very best and very worst forms can be inward-looking. Religion's finest hours have been the times when intense belief led to social transformation, yet some of its darkest days have entailed the translation of intense belief into the ruthless imposition of orthodoxy.

But the history of the United States, despite many outbreaks of prejudice and nativism, is largely a history of religion's role as a prod to social justice, inclusion, and national self-criticism. The historian Richard Wightman Fox has noted that religion can be seen "both as a democratic social power—a capacity to build community—and as a tragic perspective that acknowledges the perennial failing of human beings to make community endure."

"Religion," Fox continued, "allows people to grapple with the human mysteries that neither science nor politics can address. But it also provides a force that science and politics can call on in their effort to understand and transform the social world." For that reason alone, God and arguments about God will always have a great deal to do with the American experiment.

PART ONE

Religious Belief and Practice in the United States

2

America's Ever-Changing Religious Landscape

RICHARD N. OSTLING

THE STORY OF religion in the United States is the story of immigration. Ongoing waves of newcomers to this country, in combination with internal developments, have ensured that no nation on earth has experienced such wholesale changes in its religious makeup or had such a lavish variety of faiths from which to choose. A brief survey of the past two centuries illustrates the point and suggests no diminution of the trend in the future.

In a 1992 book, *The Churching of America: 1776–1990*, sociologists Roger Finke and Rodney Stark note that a 1776 survey of all American religious congregations found groups with British roots dominant. No big surprise there. Congregationalists boasted 668 congregations, Presbyterians 588, Baptists 497, Episcopalians 495, and Quakers 310. Those five Protestant groups accounted for nearly 80 percent of America's congregations. Following them in descending order were the German Reformed Church, Lutherans, the Dutch Reformed Church (now the Reformed Church in America), Methodists, Catholics (with 65 congregations), and Jews (with 5 synagogues).

By 1850 both immigration and internal evangelism had caused many changes. More than a third of Americans who belonged to a religious body were now Methodists (they had climbed from ninth place in 1776 to first place in 1850, mainly because of evangelism). About 21 percent of "churched" Americans were Baptists. Some 14 percent were Catholics (up from tenth place in 1776 to third place in 1850, mostly because of immigration). Presbyterians still claimed 12 percent of churchgoers but were in slow decline. Congregationalists had fallen to only 4 percent, Episcopalians to 3.5 percent. Quakers were well back in the pack.

By 1890 the top four groups had again switched places. For the first time, Catholics, with 7.3 million members, including children, claimed first place—a ranking they have kept ever since and always will, barring a massive merger among Protestant groups. Methodists followed with 7.1 million members, Baptists with 5.9 million, and Presbyterians with 1.9 million. Thirty-five years later, in 1925, Baptists had laid permanent claim to being the nation's largest Protestant denomination. Their ascendancy was due both to expansion of white Baptists and to better counting and organization of black Baptist congregations. The mostly white Southern Baptist Convention, despite its name, is represented in all fifty states and has for years been not only the largest Baptist group but the nation's largest Protestant denomination.

Now let's leap ahead to 1999. At the end of the millennium, each of two dozen religious bodies has as many local congregations as made up the whole of American religion in 1776. Table 2-1 illustrates not only the decline and fall of the colonial masters but also the rise of new denominations since colonial days and the vast variety in American religion today. Nobody knows the number of independent evangelical charismatic congregations, but the totals would be toward the top of the list.

Protestant Secularization: The Rise of the Evangelicals

The United States is noteworthy not only for the variety of its religions, but also for its high level of religiosity, which challenges the sociological theory, based on European experience, that as a society becomes more advanced, more industrial, and more technological, it will become more secular. At the time of the American Revolution about 17 percent of Americans were churched. By the Civil War, the share had grown to 37 percent. Early in this century it was just over half, and in our own generation it is more than 60 percent—some portion of which consists of merely nominal members.

America does display a different sort of secularization, according to Finke and Stark, and others. Long-established Protestant denominations tend to become more liberal in doctrine. As they do, they give rise to splits by more sectarian followers of the older tradition, or they stagnate and leave more room for emerging sectarian competitors. Since the mid-1960s, something even more radical has happened. Rather than just slowing in growth or remaining flat, some of the major "mainline" or "old-line" denominations have suffered new membership declines, year after year after year. The big losers—the Christian Church (Disciples of Christ), Episcopal Church, Presbyterian Church USA, United Church of Christ, and United Methodist Church—are generally long-established, predominately white and affluent, ecumenical and interfaith in spirit, affiliated with the National Council of Churches, and longtime leaders in college and seminary education. Relatively liberal in religion and politics, these groups have produced the leadership of business and politics and have long been considered the voice of Protestantism in what remains a heavily Protestant culture.

The mainline groups' cultural role has gradually been supplanted by the upstart conservative Protestants generally known as Evangelicals. White Evangelicals outside the National Council of Churches now outnumber white Protestants within the ecumenical fold. Without understanding this great two-party split in Protestantism, one cannot understand American religion today. It is now commonplace that the differences within a denominational family are wider and more important than the differences outside. Conservative Presbyterians have more in common with conservative Lutherans today than either has with more liberal believers carrying the same denominational label. More confusing yet, the conservative Evangelical movement consists of three sectors: entire denominations (such as the Lutheran Church-Missouri Synod), countless independent congregations, and the conservative factions within the mainline denominations.

The rising Evangelical coalition is divided in other ways. The dying Old Fundamentalists are those caught in the cultural bondage of anti-Catholicism, sometimes anti-Semitism, and in the case of Bob Jones University, of racism. The New Fundamentalists are epitomized by Jerry Falwell, who moved his flock to respectability on those points while maintaining a strictly separatist and sectarian stance. Falwell has just affiliated with the Southern Baptist Convention, which shows how solidly right wing that denomination has become. The Evangelical groups also include those too moderate to be called Fundamentalists, who have as their titular leader Billy Graham; the Pentecostal denominations, who teach the infilling of the Holy Spirit accompanied by speaking in tongues; and Charismatics, including both independent congregations and factions within mainline groups, who follow looser forms of Pentecostal practice. Black Protestantism is evangelical in many ways but is considered a separate tradition for the most part.

Since World War II, the sprawling and loosely organized conservative Evangelical movement has become the new establishment, the largest single religious faction in the United States. The Evangelicals are the innovators of American religion—in radio, television, religious movies, advertising, publishing, Christian pop and rock music, foreign mission work, seminary education, and cyberspace. Bible Belt conservatives have also shown moxie in political organizing and lobbying that far outshines that from the religious left, which cherished this field as its own for so long.

The Evangelical boom is in some ways more a story of liberal Protestant failure than conservative brilliance. As lamented by Wheaton College Professor Mark Noll in *The Scandal of the Evangelical Mind,* the Evangelicals have largely failed to create an intellectual culture with staying power over against the world views they oppose. With the exception of a handful of colleges, for example, the Evangelicals have been unable to nurture distinguished religiously based liberal arts universities as did the mainline Protestants, who invented the idea only to hand it away to secular influences.

Not Just the Protestants

The American Catholic church today is a far different church than it was in the early 1960s. From a denomination presided over by an unquestionably infallible pope and a well-disciplined clergy with no public dissent

Table 2-1. The American Religious Landscape Today

Denomination	Number of congregations
Southern Baptist Convention	40,565
United Methodist Church	36,361
National Baptist Convention, USA, Inc.	33,000
Roman Catholic Church	22,728
Church of God in Christ	15,300
Churches of Christ	14,000
Assemblies of God	11,884
Presbyterian Church USA	11,328
C.o.J.C.o. Latter-day Saints	11,000
Evangelical Lutheran Church in America	10,396
Jehovah's Witnesses	10,671
African Methodist Episcopal Church	8,000
Episcopal Church	7,415
United Church of Christ	6,110
Lutheran Church – Missouri Synod	6,099
Church of God (Tennessee)	6,060
American Baptist Churches	5,839
(Independent) Christian Churches	5,579
Church of the Nazarene	5,135
Seventh Day Adventist Church	4,363
Christian Church (Disciples of Christ)	3,840
United Pentecostal Church	3,790
Baptist Bible Fellowship	3,600
Jewish congregations (all denominations)	3,416

and characterized by a venerable liturgy, recited in Latin, with weekly attendance expected of all, it has become a federation of internally divided quasi denominations. What began in the 1960s with a seemingly modest effort of reform at the Second Vatican Council has ended with every aspect of Catholic tradition under question, and the questioners under question by a rigorous pope and his Vatican staff. America's biggest single denomination is now a federation of fiefdoms consisting of the loyalists and the liberals, the divorced and remarried, the alienated and the indifferent, the merely ethnic or "communal Catholics," and the "cafeteria Catholics" who pick and choose what to practice. Public opinion surveys show that people who identify as Catholic are more liberal on sexual morals than Protestants as a whole. Birth rates and opinions on abortion are virtually the same. Like Protestantism, the American Catholic Church today seems to be many denominations, loosely united.

In Judaism, perhaps the biggest development is the aging and shrinking of its population base. Younger American Jews marrying Gentiles are now a majority for the first time in history. The Jewish population study of 1990 shows that children of these mixed marriages are least likely to receive a Jewish upbringing, more likely to be educated into Christianity—but most likely to receive no religious education and to carry no religious identification into adulthood. Recently we had two cries of alarm, one from Alan Dershowitz on the secular left and the other from Elliott Abrams on the religious right, saying American Judaism is in mortal danger unless it somehow provides a new identity to the younger generation.

What about Everybody Else?

A topic of considerable controversy among experts on American religion is the number of Americans who belong to religions other than Christianity and Judaism. In 1989 and 1990 City University of New York researchers put a religious identification question on a random telephone marketing survey and got data for 113,000 U.S. households. Their estimate was that there were 527,000 Muslims, 401,000 Buddhists, and 227,000 Hindus in the United States. By contrast, the *1998 Encyclopedia Britannica Book of the Year* puts the numbers at 3.8 million Muslims, 1.9 million Buddhists, and almost 800,000 Hindus. And needless to say, if you ask publicists for the Muslims, Hindus, or Buddhists, they will give you estimates vastly bigger than the *Britannica* does. Two special factors affect new and immigrant faiths. First, they may lack organizational infrastructure that relates to specific religious congregations. For example, despite estimates of millions of U.S. Muslims, only a thousand or so mosques and community centers exist to serve them. And for Buddhists and Hindus, the whole idea of congregations and denominations and memberships is alien to Asian tradition.

However we count them, there is no doubt that immigrants are now, as before, gradually changing the face of American religion. President Lyndon Johnson's signing of the 1965 Immigration and Nationality Act, the first major change in law since 1924, greatly facilitated entry by Asians. Buddhism and Hinduism are now firmly rooted in America, and Islam has the potential to rival or surpass Judaism as the nation's second-ranking religion if institutions and leaders to serve them can be found.

Islam faces the same challenge as Judaism with the influx from Eastern Europe toward the end of the nineteenth century. New-style congregations had to be invented, new buildings built, and new schools started to train a new type of rabbi. U.S. Islam is just beginning to create the communal organizations that have served Judaism so well. There is no coherent association of mosques to unite immigrants with native-born blacks, and national organizations of other types are young. Muslims are divided the way Protestants have been, by ethnicity, race, and language. Only in 1996 did U.S. Muslims establish a school for training clergy at the graduate level to parallel the Jewish and Christian seminaries.

Another future trend to note is the large and growing minority of younger Americans who define themselves as "spiritual" but not "religious," signaling a quest that is neither limited by nor nurtured by the traditional organized religions of the past. More than any previous generation, Americans age eighteen and under are thoroughly detached from traditional Christian concepts. By and large they do not believe Jesus is the unique savior of mankind, do not read the Bible as God's word, and do not accept the idea of moral absolutes. Whether one views that as progress or regress depends on one's own concepts of Christianity, reality, and the cosmos. But it is certainly another revolution in our time.

Futurists are telling us that the old ways of doing religion in America cannot last. Younger Americans have increasingly short attention spans, so that one California church changes the elements of worship every eight to ten minutes—a development that sounds the death knell of the sermon. We're told young Americans are increasingly unable to read printed material—a body blow to Protestant religion as we've known it. They say youth distrusts traditional institutions, among which the church and synagogue are the most traditional of all. Some few are pronouncing even the decline of local congregations in favor of informal house churches or cyberchurches linked only randomly by computer or totally individual behaviors.

Those who look to the churches for the salvation of civic life or for the renovation of politics should realize that organized religion will have its hands full coping with purely internal issues in the coming generation.

3

America's Changing Political and Moral Values

ROBERT J. BLENDON, JOHN M. BENSON,
MOLLYANN BRODIE, DREW E. ALTMAN,
RICHARD MORIN, CLAUDIA DEANE,
AND NINA KJELLSON

As WE ENTER a new century, it is a good time to examine how the nation's political and moral values have changed in the past thirty years and how Democrats and Republicans differ today on some important values. During the summer and fall of 1998, we conducted three polls to look at these two issues, as well as Americans' views on religion in the public domain. We found that Americans today are generally more conservative in their views on the role of government and more concerned about the country's moral decline than they were thirty years ago.

The 1990s

Table 3-1 sets out differences in Americans' values during the 1960s and today. During the 1960s only a distinct minority of Americans was distrustful of government; today two-thirds of Americans could be so categorized, trusting the government in Washington to do the right thing "only some of the time" or "never." The proportion of Americans who see big government—as opposed to big labor or big business—as the biggest threat

Table 3-1. American Values, Then and Now

	Then	Now (1998)
Role of government		
Trust government in Washington to do the right thing only some of the time or never	(1964) 23%	66%
Big government is biggest threat to the future of the country	(1965) 35%	59%
Government has gone too far in regulating business and interfering with the free enterprise system	(1964) 43%	59%
Prefer smaller government with fewer services to larger government with more/many services	(1976) 40%	59%
Would like government to do more to help minority groups	(1968) 50%	37%
(Government should/It is the responsibility of government to) reduce differences in income	(1973) 48%	30%
Favor death penalty for persons convicted of murder	(1966) 42%	69%
Morality and toleration		
Young people today do not have as strong a sense of right and wrong as they did 50 years ago	(1965) 46%	78%
People in general today do not lead lives as honest and moral as they used to	(1965) 52%	71%
Homosexuals should have equal rights in terms of job opportunities	(1977) 56%	87%
Approve of marriage between Jews and non-Jews	(1968) 58%	75%
There should not be laws against marriage between (negroes/blacks/African-Americans) and whites (response of whites)	(1963) 36%	(1996) 87%
If your party nominated well-qualified person for president who was an atheist, would vote for that person	(1958) 18%	44%

Source: See text.

to the country's future has grown from 35 percent in the 1960s to 59 percent today. Thirty years ago Americans were pretty evenly divided over whether the government should provide special help to minorities and whether it had a responsibility to reduce income differences. Today only 37 percent would like government to do more to help minorities, and only 30 percent believe government should help reduce differences in income. In fact, of the issues we tested, the only power Americans are more willing to invest in their government today than they were thirty years ago is the power to administer the death penalty for persons convicted of murder.

Americans are also more worried about moral values than they were thirty years ago. In 1952 only 34 percent of Americans thought that young people of their time did not have as strong a sense of right and wrong as young people did fifty years earlier. In 1965 fewer than half of poll respondents embraced that negative view of young Americans. But today 78 percent feel that the morals of young Americans have declined. Indeed, 71 percent believe that people in general lead less honest and moral lives than they once did.

Another striking change since the 1960s is that Americans today express much more tolerant views of different groups in society. Approval of marriage between Jews and non-Jews rose from 59 percent in 1968 to 75 percent in 1998. Even more dramatically, the proportion of whites who believe there should not be laws against marriages between African Americans and whites rose from 36 percent to 87 percent. As late as 1977, not much more than half of Americans thought homosexuals should have equal rights in terms of job opportunities; today 87 percent support equal job opportunities. Americans have also become more tolerant of atheists. Though a majority are still unwilling to vote for an atheist for president, the share that is willing to do so increased from 18 percent in 1958 to 44 percent today.

Partisan Differences

Republicans are clearly the party of limited government, though close to half of Democrats polled are also skeptical of "big government" (table 3-2).

Table 3-2. Role of Government Today: Differences between
Republicans and Democrats

	Republicans	Democrats
Big government is biggest threat to the future of the country	70%	47%
Government has gone too far in regulating business and interfering with the free enterprise system	72%	52%
Prefer smaller government with fewer services to larger government with many services–	73%	47%
and feel strongly	50%	20%
Would like government to do more to help minority groups	23%	52%
Disagree that we have gone too far in pushing equal rights	43%	64%
Support affirmative action programs that give preference to minorities	21%	43%
It is responsibility of government to reduce differences in income	20%	43%
It is government's responsibility to improve standard of living of all Americans	38%	65%
Favor death penalty for persons convicted of murder	76%	60%

Source: See text.

Considerably more Democrats than Republicans are favorably inclined toward specific government programs, such as aid to minorities and support for equal rights. Twice as many Democrats as Republicans (though still a minority of Democrats) support affirmative action. Far more Democrats than Republicans (but, again, still a minority of Democrats) believe government should reduce differences in income; a strong majority of Democrats (compared with only 38 percent of Republicans) believes it is the government's responsibility to improve the living standard of all Americans.

When the issues become focused on morality and toleration, other discrepancies between the parties arise (table 3-3). Although strong majori-

Table 3-3. Morality, Toleration, and Religion in the Public Domain Today: Differences between Republicans and Democrats

	Republicans	Democrats
Belief that morality is declining		
Young people today do not have as strong a sense of right and wrong as they did 50 years ago	80%	75%
People in general today do not lead lives as honest and moral as they used to	78%	68%
Values and moral beliefs in this country have gotten pretty seriously off on the wrong track	83%	65%
Toleration of groups in society		
Homosexuals should have equal rights in terms of job opportunities	84%	88%
Approve of marriage between Jews and non-Jews	75%	77%
There should not be laws against marriages between (blacks/African-Americans) and whites	86%	85%
If your party nominated well-qualified person for president who was an atheist, would vote for that person	35%	41%
Toleration of behaviors		
Agree strongly that Americans are too tolerant and accepting of behaviors that in the past were considered immoral or wrong	55%	34%
Agree that the world is changing and we need to adjust our morals	33%	50%
Is acceptable behavior. . .		
Having a child without being married	47%	62%
Having sex before marriage	45%	60%
Having an abortion	42%	56%
Sex between two adults of the same sex	16%	31%
Disagree that divorce should be harder to obtain	24%	41%
President as moral example		
The president has a greater responsibility than leaders of other organizations to set an example with his personal life	69%	26%

(Table continues)

Table 3-3 *(continued)*

	Republicans	Democrats
Support for religion in public domain		
Would like to see religious and spiritual values have a greater influence in politics and public life	48%	36%
It is important for organized religious groups to stand up for their beliefs in politics	61%	49%
It is sometimes right for clergymen to discuss political candidates or issues from the pulpit	40%	29%
Government should take specific steps to protect America's religious heritage	55%	46%
Religious people must take political action to protect their rights	63%	55%

Source: See text.

ties in both parties see morality in America on the decline and are tolerant of different groups in our society, Republicans are substantially less tolerant of certain behaviors than are Democrats. Three behaviors in particular divide Republicans and Democrats: having a child without being married, having sexual relations before marriage, and having an abortion. In each case a majority of Republicans finds the behavior unacceptable, while a majority of Democrats believe it is acceptable. A small minority of both parties (31 percent of Democrats, 16 percent of Republicans) approves of sex between two adults of the same sex. The two parties also agree that divorce should be harder to obtain.

The role of the president in setting a moral example sharply splits the parties. The long-running controversy over President Clinton's affair with Monica Lewinsky is undoubtedly part of the reason for the divide, but the partisan positions are generally in tune with attitudes expressed on other issues of moral behavior. Republicans express stronger support than Democrats for religion in the public domain. Forty-eight percent of Republicans, but only 36 percent of Democrats, would like to see religious and spiritual values have a greater influence in politics and public life.

A majority of both parties (63 percent of Republicans, 55 percent of Democrats) believe that religious people must take political action to protect their rights; 61 percent of Republicans and 49 percent of Democrats believe it is important for organized religious groups to stand up for their beliefs in politics; and 55 percent of Republicans and 46 percent of Democrats believe government should take specific steps to protect America's religious heritage. Minorities of both parties (40 percent of Republicans, 29 percent of Democrats) think it is sometimes right for clergymen to discuss political candidates or issues from the pulpit.

Polls Used

The current results reported here are drawn from three polls in a special series conducted by the *Washington Post*/Henry J. Kaiser Family Foundation/Harvard University survey project, July 29–August 18, 1998; August 10–27, 1998; and November 13–17, 1998. Other data come from polls by Ben Gaffin and Associates (1952); the Gallup Poll (1958, 1965, 1966, 1968, 1977); Gallup/Potomac Associates (1964); the National Election Survey (1964); Gallup/*Catholic Digest* (1965); Trendex/General Electric (1968); the National Opinion Research Center (1963,1973,1996); and CBS News/*New York Times* (1976). Results of all polls cited may be obtained from the Roper Center for Public Opinion Research, Storrs, Connecticut. The work of analyzing the polls was supported by the Henry J. Kaiser Family Foundation. The views expressed are solely those of the authors, and no official endorsement by the Kaiser Family Foundation is intended or should be inferred.

4

The Conservative Protestant Family
Traditional Rhetoric, Progressive Practice

W. BRADFORD WILCOX AND
JOHN P. BARTKOWSKI

CONVENTIONAL WISDOM suggests that evangelical Protestantism is a uniform force for reaction in American life. Indeed, the close ties between conservative Protestants—that is, Protestants who take a high view of the Bible and prioritize evangelism—and the political right give some credence to this view. James Dobson, Gary Bauer, and Pat Robertson, leaders of family ministries and political groups loosely associated with conservative Protestantism, consistently push the Republican Party to stake out conservative stands on social issues. At the grassroots level, white conservative Protestants (who make up almost 20 percent of the population) have migrated at disproportionate levels to the Republican Party, to the point where they are almost 50 percent more likely than other Americans to identify as Republicans.

Conservative Protestantism's links to political conservatism grow largely out of its more fundamental concern with the preservation of the "traditional" family. In recent years, conservative Protestant churches and ministries like Promise Keepers have produced a steady stream of sermons, books, videos, and radio programs designed to help conservative Protestants "focus on the family." Here again, the conservative Protestant message appears uniformly conservative. In 1998, the Southern Baptist Convention, the largest denomination in the conservative Protestant tradition, passed a resolution calling on wives to "submit" to their husbands. Conservative Protestant parenting experts, led by Dobson, president of Focus on the Family, are some of the culture's most vociferous defenders of a traditional disciplinary child-rearing style that incorporates corporal punishment.[1] And more than 85 percent of conservative Protestants believe that "the husband should be the head of the family," compared with 48 percent of all other Americans, according to the 1996 Pew-funded Religious Identity and Influence Survey.

The conservative family rhetoric and attitudes issuing from conservative Protestant quarters have prompted a vigorous response from feminists and mainstream media. Patricia Ireland, president of the National Organization of Women, accused the Promise Keepers of being "religious political extremists" bent on keeping women in the "back seat."[2] Journalists Cokie and Steve Roberts suggested that the Southern Baptist position on marital submission "can clearly lead to abuse, both physical and emotional."[3] Conservative Protestant leaders have responded in kind. For instance, Dobson recently wrote that "conservative Christians continue to lose ground in the great civil war of values... [as] the cultural elites... continue their campaign to marginalize and paralyze us."[4]

Beyond the rhetorical volleys that characterize this elite-driven cultural conflict, however, the reality is that family practice of conservative Protestants on the ground confounds the denunciations of left-leaning cultural elites and the proscriptions of conservative Protestant elites. What we call the "conservative Protestant family paradox" is best summarized as follows: conservative Protestant family practice doesn't match conservative Protestant family rhetoric. When it comes to the *practice* of family life, conservative Protestant men and women act in ways that parallel or are in fact more progressive than other Americans.

First, conservative Protestants approach married life in ways that largely mirror the practices of other Americans. Melinda Lundquist and Christian Smith, researchers at the University of North Carolina, find *no* difference between conservative Protestants and other Americans in marital decisions dealing with family finances, childrearing, and work decisions.[5] Our own research indicates that there are also no differences in patterns of male household labor—that is, cooking, cleaning, and so on—between conservative Protestant and other American couples. We also find, contrary to the argument by Cokie and Steve Roberts, no evidence that conservative Protestant men are more likely to abuse their wives physically.

The only exceptions to this general pattern of conservative Protestant marital similarity are that conservative Protestants are more likely to report that husbands take the "lead in spiritual matters," according to Lundquist and Smith; that conservative Protestant men *and* women are more likely to report higher levels of marital satisfaction than other Americans, according to our research; and that conservative Protestant men are more likely to be empathetic and affectionate toward their wives, according to our research. Thus, despite conservative gender role rhetoric and attitudes to the contrary, the day-to-day reality of conservative Protestant marriages doesn't seem all that different from the lived experience of other American couples. Indeed, the expressive marital style of conservative Protestant men seems more progressive than that of other American men.

Moreover, when it comes to parenting, conservative Protestants—especially conservative Protestant men—are in many ways more progressive than other Americans. The single exception to this pattern is that conservative Protestant parents spank their toddlers and preschoolers more often than other parents, according to a research team led by Christopher Ellison at the University of Texas.[6] However, the kind of warm, expressive parenting style first pushed by Dr. Spock is also deeply entrenched in this subculture. We find that conservative Protestant mothers praise and hug their children more often than do other mothers. More surprisingly, we also find that conservative Protestant fathers are more likely to practice this kind of expressive parenting.

In fact, conservative Protestant fathers are more involved with their children than other fathers. They have dinner with their children and volunteer for youth activities like soccer and Scouts more than other fathers. Conservative Protestant fathers are also more amenable to doing their part to take up the inevitable supervisory tasks associated with school-aged children. Conservative Protestant fathers report monitoring their children's chores, homework, and TV-watching regimen more closely than other fathers. And conservative Protestant fathers are no more or less likely than other fathers to share basic childcare tasks with their wives, like feeding, clothing, and bathing preschoolers.

In many ways, then, conservative Protestant men more closely resemble the iconic new father of the 1990s—that is, the expressive, involved, and egalitarian family man—than do other men. This development is particularly surprising in light of an observation made by Ralph LaRossa, a sociologist at Georgia State: "Yes, fatherhood has changed if one looks at the culture of fatherhood—the ideologies surrounding men's parenting. No, fatherhood has not changed (at least significantly), if one looks at the conduct of fatherhood—how fathers behave vis-à-vis their children."[7]

LaRossa's point is that even as men and women's gender role attitudes have become markedly more progressive, the behavior of American fathers is not that different from the way it was twenty or thirty years ago. So, why is it that a religious culture that has championed gender role traditionalism is to a large degree leading the way in active male familial involvement, as well as an expressive approach to marriage and parenting among men? In other words, what explains the conservative Protestant family paradox?

In part, the standard sociological explanations can help us unravel this puzzle. Duane Alwin at the University of Michigan has tied the erosion of distinctive patterns of childrearing and fertility among Catholics to their dramatic post-1950s socioeconomic mobility.[8] Something similar is probably happening among conservative Protestants. For instance, from 1972 to 1994, the percentage of conservative Protestant college graduates more than doubled from 8 to 18 percent; over the same period, the percentage of conservative Protestant high-school dropouts fell from 44 to 18 percent. Thus, conservative Protestants may be more likely to encounter and adopt conventional middle-class family behavior regarding marriage and childrearing. This helps account for the fact that conservative Protestants are not very different from other Americans in their patterns of marital decisionmaking, housework, and basic childcare. Still, socioeconomic mobility doesn't explain why conservative Protestants outpace their peers when it comes to expressive parenting, higher levels of paternal involvement, and more expressive male behavior in marriage—

particularly since they remain slightly less educated and well heeled than other Americans.

The warm, expressive character of evangelical parenting and marriage appears, in part, to be an outgrowth of the increasingly therapeutic character of American evangelicalism more generally. From stadiums filled with Promise Keepers men weeping over their sins to mega-churches offering small groups for every imaginable emotional need, conservative Protestant institutions have turned their attention in a dramatic way to the psychological well-being of their members. The expressive ethos produced in conservative Protestant churches has undoubtedly carried over into the family, which helps to explain why mothers and fathers in this subculture are more likely to hug and praise their children and why men are more likely to be affectionate and empathetic to their wives.

However, the distinctive parenting style among evangelicals also seems related to the way they have connected notions of "divinely ordained" authority to family life. In sermons, books, small groups, and radio programs, evangelical institutions like Focus on the Family press the message that the family can be saved if parents exercise authority in a way that models the love of God. Moreover, fathers are expressly told that they have a crucial role to play. As one conservative Protestant parenting expert said, "Is Dad necessary? You bet he is! He is part of a God-designed team and his teamwork is essential to the personal growth of his children."[9] This focus on the proper exercise of family authority—including paternal authority, allied with the distinctively powerful social supports and controls at the disposal of conservative Protestant churches, appears to be a critical factor in accounting for the progressive parental practices of conservative Protestants.

But why doesn't this powerful family focus translate into more differences in marital behavior, given the conservative gender rhetoric and attitudes found among conservative Protestants? Part of the reason for this gap between culture and conduct can be attributed to the shifting ideal of authority in conservative Protestantism. In recent years, partly as a consequence of feminist pressures within and outside of the conservative Protestant subculture, the ideal of male authority has evolved from one of "headship" to "servant-leadership." This discursive innovation allows conservative Protestant men and women to retain their allegiance to the symbolic authority of men even as they adopt behaviors more in keeping with the norms of their nonconservative Protestant friends, neighbors, and co-workers. Moreover, it allows conservative Protestants to express—symbolically if not practically—their moral superiority over these very same nonconservative Protestant friends, neighbors, and coworkers. In fact, its emphasis on male leadership is precisely the kind of symbolic boundary-work that lends conservative Protestantism its distinctive religious strength, as Christian Smith argues in his recent book, *American Evangelicalism: Embattled and Thriving.*[10]

Finally, this emphasis on male authority is clearly tied to notions of male familial responsibility in this subculture. Conservative Protestantism appears to offer men the symbolic gift of "servant-leadership" in return for demanding greater involvement in the home and more expressive behavior with their wives. In fact, our research indicates that the conservative Protestant couples with the most traditional gender role attitudes are the couples where the wives express the most satisfaction with their husband's empathy and affection.

Conservative Protestants and their critics—from mainstream media to feminists—may give the impression that conservative Protestants are stalwart agents of reaction in American life. But the reality of the "conservative Protestant family paradox" is that conservative Protestants are, in fact, not that different from other Americans when it comes to marital practice and more progressive when it comes to parenting, especially fathering. This paradox suggests that conservative Protestant leaders should pay more attention to the marital practice of their own rank and file before attacking "cultural elites." But it also suggests that their critics, ironically enough, might learn a thing or two about family life from average conservative Protestants.

PART TWO
Politics and Witness

5

A *Screwtape Letter* for the Twenty-First Century
What a Senior Devil Might Think about Religion and Politics

PETER WEHNER

In 1942 the Christian writer and Oxford don C. S. Lewis wrote one of his most influential books, The Screwtape Letters, *in which a senior devil, Screwtape, instructs a junior devil, Wormwood, in the art of temptation. Lewis's intent was to illuminate matters having to do with faith, life, and human folly by writing about the Christian faith from the perspective of the Devil (thus God is spoken of as "the Enemy"). This chapter contemplates what both Professor Lewis and Screwtape might say about religion and politics in our time.*

I AM RECRUITING you to do our work in a target-rich environment: politics. It is true that the Enemy has sometimes used politics to advance what He foolishly cares about—things like "justice" and "human dignity," "righteousness" and "mercy." But the good news for us is that being actively involved in politics without being seduced by it can be difficult—and human folly and egoism strongly work in our favor. As long as your patients remain oblivious to the snares of worldliness, they become unwitting instruments in our cause.

As you surely know by now, one of the best ways to undermine Christian faith and good works is to act insidiously. Avoid a direct assault on faith; it gives the Enemy's followers time to prepare for the assault and respond. If we succeed in directly planting doubt in the mind of believers, they often go to their knees in prayer, humbly asking the Enemy for strength. When that happens we have lost them. A better strategy is to cloud reality. Keep Christians from realizing what is involved. We want them to think they're doing the work of the Enemy while they are in fact advancing our ends. This approach is much more effective—and much more amusing to watch.

The following methods are ones I have found to be particularly useful.

—1. Rely on omissions, distortions, and outright lies. These are among the sharpest arrows in our quiver. The key is to disfigure the original meaning and context of the Enemy's play book (they refer to it as the "Bible"). Here are some historical facts that you must continually obscure. First, Christ (the son of the Enemy) and His disciples were profoundly mistrustful of power, and His earthly ministry was directed against the pretensions of earthly power. He came to the world as a lowly servant and never became a political leader. In worldly terms, His disciples had no status or influence, and neither Christ nor His disciples led a political movement of any kind. Indeed, their most sacred symbol, the cross, is an emblem of agony and humiliation that is the antithesis of worldly power and victory. From our perspective it is just as well for Christians to acknowledge these things without taking them seriously. Let them pay lip service, for nominal faith is as good as no faith at all. Your task is to so thoroughly twist your patients' understanding of Christ's kingdom that they actually come to believe that by forming coalitions, networking among the politically powerful, writing laws to advance His "social agenda," and securing "a place at the table," they are following in His footsteps.

—2. Promote ugly division among believers. One reason why politics is such rich ground for us is that it breeds acrimonious debate among followers of the Enemy. As you know by now, politics often inflames human emotions like anger, bitterness, resentment. What could be better for our cause than getting followers of the Enemy on different sides of an issue? What great fun it is to watch them spit venom! Can you imagine my joy when one prominent religious-political figure—he even has the title "Reverend"—accused fellow believers with whom he has political disagreements of being a strong force in Nazi Germany! We must always discourage reasoned and civil debate since it can eventually be turned against us and become an instrument for ascertaining "truth." What we are after is argument by invective (preferably accompanied by sloppy reasoning).

Christians will deny it, of course, but behind closed doors and in the privacy of their own political offices, on telephone lines, and in "off the record" comments, these "brothers" in the faith will savage one another. Sometimes they do it even when they're on the same side of an issue! These clanging cymbals not only make for great fun—they do our work for us. Their hypocrisy makes the "unbelievers" whom the Enemy is trying to win over wary and cynical. So long as political passions undermine such contemptible "virtues" as love, humility, forgiveness, forbearance, kindness, and mercy, we have accomplished our goals.

—3. Take advantage of the messianic illusion. What you want Christians to believe is that their work is absolutely necessary if the Enemy is to accomplish His goals on earth. Make them think they are indispensable. Do you see why this is so important? Because if Christians believe everything depends on them, they will develop an aggressive, anxious, even desperate spirit. They will show little grace toward others. They will begin to believe that only they and a few of their kind are strong enough to resist "compromise." And they will disdain fellow believers who do not share their zeal for their cause. The most delicious quarry are those Christians who believe that at stake in their work is nothing less than the influence of Christianity in America. They actually believe Christ depends on them instead of the other way around, which is the surest road to vainglory.

—4. Rely on worldliness. Although the Christian church has often thrived under persecution, it has been corrupted virtually every time it seizes power or becomes closely aligned with power. The reason, of course, is that more often than not Christians in positions of worldly authority don't transform the world; they are conformed to it. You would think that by now this would be widely understood. Thankfully, it isn't. Here, then, is the dirty little secret we must keep confidential, lest the followers of the Enemy learn from it: religious leaders are easily seduced by political power. Allow these shameless namedroppers access to worldly power and they make sure everybody knows about it. For all their rants against worldliness, they are like children with their faces pressed against a toy store window, longing to get in. That's their Achilles heel.

One particularly troublesome Christian once wrote that he was a proud member of a political movement. He rationalized that surely the Enemy must approve what he was doing since he was (in this instance) opposing an unjust war. Except that the political movement, whatever its ideals, did a good deal of hating. Christ became subordinate to movement goals. That is exactly what we want to see happen. So we must continue to press the point that religion ought to be an instrument of political ideology. A means to an end. If we succeed in getting Christian witness sacrificed at the altar of politics, we win—regardless of the merits of the particular political issue. I'm willing to lose a vote on H.R. 666 to win souls.

—5. Lack of theological integrity. Many Christians explain their involvement in politics as a way to advance the Enemy's agenda in the public arena, and they begin with good intentions. How should we respond? Our goal is to get them to bend the Bible to conform to their political predispositions, so that their political agenda (pursued in the name of Christ) has little or no relation to what He says. I call it cafeteria-style theology, in which His followers arbitrarily pick and choose the issues they care about. As you'll see, this works wonders.

Let me give you a specific example. The Enemy's "New Testament" play book says a staggering amount about riches, more than about almost any other subject. What is said is almost always in the nature of a warning. The reason, of course, is that the Enemy knows the damage we can do to His followers through riches: the danger they pose to one's soul, the pull of worldliness, the corruption of affections. What I most detest, and what I most fear, are earnest followers who take the Enemy's words to heart, who meditate on them, and, worst of all, who act on them. Those people are a lost cause.

But don't despair. There are plenty of others. For them, our aim is to obscure the real appeal of their faith—its absolute otherness. We must patiently erase the realization that the Enemy has chosen the weak things of the world to shame the strong; that His power is made perfect in weakness; that they must die to live; that the meek and not the strong shall inherit the earth; that they are called to be servants and not masters; and that they are called to love and not hate their enemies.

—How do we avert their attention from warnings the Enemy has put in bright neon light? Remind them of the weight of the Enemy's demands.

Whisper in their ear that these precepts should not be taken literally. Have them strive for "relevance" instead of faithfulness. Encourage them to reinterpret the words of Christ. Once you've done all that you can, watch while those who insist that the words of Christ ought to be a guide to political action become silent on issues of such obvious concern to Him and speak out on issues He cares little or nothing about. It's bad for them, and it's bad for their witness. But it's good, very good, for us.

I close by reminding you of a crucial distinction. Getting followers of the Enemy involved in politics is not enough; it can even redound to His glory (I am thinking here of contemptible figures like William Wilberforce and his efforts to end British slave trade). No, what we have to do is coax them into a cul-de-sac of human ego, blind hubris, love of power. Once they become involved in politics, we want to corrupt them—but it is best to do it a little at a time. Do I need to explain why patience will be rewarded? Surely you are familiar with the "frog's dilemma." If you drop a frog in boiling water it will jump out, but if you heat the water slowly, the frog will adjust and accommodate itself to the new temperature until it finally burns to death. We want to turn up the temperature of political activism slowly but steadily. Surely you have learned enough by now to agree with me that the best sport is to take a bad thing (carefully thinking through the social implications of faith) and turn it into a good thing (political idolatry).

Finally, to anticipate the Enemy's strategy, we must consider His aims. What He cares about are all those things for which we have utter contempt: good works, purity of heart, a joyful spirit, grace, the habit of obedience even during moments of doubt, winning converts by practical demonstrations of love (remember, we want to encourage abstract pronouncements of love and compassion; our undoing is when Christians demonstrate real love and compassion for people in need). The Enemy always does terrible damage to us when His followers believe deep in their hearts that they are citizens of heaven and not of earth. It is then, paradoxically, that they do the most good here on earth, both within and beyond politics. Do not let this old Christian truth be revealed, my dear Wormwood, or else we're finished.

Your affectionate uncle,
SCREWTAPE

6

First Trombone

TAYLOR BRANCH

Take him, Lord—this morning—
Wash him with hyssop inside and out,
Hang him up and drain him dry of sin. . . .
Fill him full of the dynamite of thy power,
Anoint him all over with the oil of thy salvation
And set his tongue on fire.

JAMES WELDON JOHNSON, *God's Trombones*

LATE IN THE afternoon of Thursday, December 1, 1955, Rosa Parks was arrested in Montgomery, Alabama, for refusing to give up her seat on a public city bus to a white passenger. Over the weekend, leaders of the black community organized a bus boycott to begin on Monday morning. On Monday afternoon, December 5, Martin Luther King, Jr., the young pastor of Montgomery's Dexter Avenue Baptist Church, was chosen to lead the ongoing boycott and to speak at a mass meeting that evening at the Holt Street Baptist Church. King had less than half an hour to prepare his first political address.

King stood silently for a moment. When he greeted the enormous crowd of strangers, who were packed in the balconies and aisles, peering in through the windows and upward from seats on the floor, he spoke in a deep voice, stressing his diction in a slow introductory cadence. "We are here this evening—for serious business," he said, in even pulses, rising and then

46

falling in pitch. When he paused, only one or two "yes" responses came up from the crowd, and they were quiet ones. It was a throng of shouters, he could see, but they were waiting to see where he would take them. "We are here in a general sense, because first and foremost—we are American citizens—and we are determined to apply our citizenship—to the fullness of its means," he said. "But we are here in a specific sense—because of the bus situation in Montgomery." A general murmur of assent came back to him, and the pitch of King's voice rose gradually through short, quickened sentences. "The situation is not at all new. The problem has existed over endless years. Just the other day—just last Thursday to be exact—one of the finest citizens in Montgomery—not one of the finest Negro citizens—but one of the finest citizens in Montgomery—was taken from a bus and carried to jail and arrested—because she refused to give up—to give her seat to a white person."

The crowd punctuated each pause with scattered "Yeses" and "Amens." They were with him in rhythm, but lagged slightly behind in enthusiasm. Then King spoke of the law, saying that the arrest was doubtful even under the segregation ordinances, because reserved Negro and white bus sections were not specified in them. "The law has never been clarified at that point," he said, drawing an emphatic "Hell, no" from one man in his audience. "And I think I speak with—with legal authority—not that I have any legal authority—but I think I speak with legal authority behind me—that the law—the ordinance—the city ordinance has never been totally clarified." This sentence marked King as a speaker who took care with distinctions, but it took the crowd nowhere. King returned to the special nature of Rosa Parks. "And since it had to happen, I'm happy it happened to a person like Mrs. Parks," he said, "for nobody can doubt the boundless outreach of her integrity. Nobody can doubt the height of her character, nobody can doubt the depth of her Christian commitment." That's right, a soft chorus answered. "And just because she refused to get up, she was arrested," King repeated. The crowd was stirring now, following King at the speed of a medium walk.

He paused slightly longer. "And you know, my friends, there comes a time," he cried, "when people get tired of being trampled over by the iron feet of oppression." A flock of "Yeses" was coming back at him when suddenly the individual responses dissolved into a rising cheer and applause exploded beneath the cheer—all within the space of a second. The startling noise rolled on and on, like a wave that refused to break, and just when it seemed that the roar must finally weaken, a wall of sound came in from the enormous crowd outdoors to push the volume still higher. Thunder seemed to be added to the lower register—the sound of feet stomping on the wooden floor until the loudness became something that was not so much heard as it was sensed by vibrations in the lungs. The giant cloud of noise shook the building and refused to go away. One sentence had set it loose somehow, pushing the call—and—response of the Negro church service past the din of a political rally and on to something else that King had never known before. There was a rabbit of awesome proportions in those bushes. As the noise finally fell back, King's voice rose above it to fire again. "There comes a time, my friends, when people get tired of being thrown across the abyss of humiliation, where they experience the bleakness of nagging despair," he declared. "There comes a time when people get tired of being pushed out of the glittering sunlight of life's July, and left standing amidst the piercing chill of an Alpine November." King was making a new run, but the crowd drowned him out. No one could tell whether the roar came in response to the nerve he had touched, or simply out of pride in a speaker from whose tongue such rhetoric rolled so easily. "We are here—we are here because we are tired now," King repeated.

Perhaps daunted by the power that was bursting forth from the crowd, King moved quickly to address the pitfalls of a boycott. "Now let us say that we are not here advocating violence," he said. "We have overcome that." A man in the crowd shouted "Repeat that! Repeat that!" "I want it to be known throughout Montgomery and throughout this nation that we are Christian people," said King, putting three distinct syllables in "Christian." "The only weapon that we have in our hands this evening is the weapon of protest." There was a crisp shout of approval right on the beat of King's pause. He and the audience moved into a slow trot. "If we were incarcerated behind the iron curtains of a communistic nation—we couldn't do this. If we were trapped in the dungeon of a totalitarian regime—we couldn't do this. But the great glory of American democracy is the right to protest for right." When the shouts of approval died down, King rose up with his final reason to avoid violence, which was to distinguish themselves from their opponents in the Klan and the White Citizens Council. "There will be no crosses burned at any bus stops in Montgomery," he said. "There will be no white persons pulled out of their homes and taken out on some distant road and murdered. There will be nobody among us who will stand up and defy the Constitution of this nation."

King paused. The church was quiet but it was humming. "My friends," he said slowly, "I want it to be known—that we're going to work with grim and bold determination—to gain justice on the buses in this city. And we are not wrong. We are not wrong in what we are doing." There was a muffled shout of anticipation, as the crowd sensed that King was moving closer to the heart of his cause. "If we are wrong—the Supreme Court of this nation is wrong," King sang out. He was rocking now, his voice seeming to be at once deep and high pitched. "If we are wrong—God Almighty is wrong!" he shouted, and the crowd seemed to explode a second time, as it had done when he said they were tired. Wave after wave of noise broke over them, cresting into the farthest reaches of the ceiling. They were far beyond Rosa Parks or the bus laws. King's last cry had fused blasphemy to the edge of his faith and the heart of theirs. The noise swelled until King cut through it to move past a point of unbearable tension. "If we are wrong Jesus of Nazareth was merely a utopian dreamer and never came down to earth! If we are wrong justice is a lie." This was too much. He had to wait some time before delivering his soaring conclusion, in a flight of anger mixed with rapture: "And we are determined here in Montgomery—to work and fight until justice runs down like water, and righteousness like a mighty stream!" The audience all but smothered this passage from Amos, the lowly herdsman prophet of Israel who, along with the priestly Isaiah, was King's favorite biblical authority on justice.

He backed off the emotion to speak of the need for unity, the dignity of protest, the historical precedent of the labor movement. Comparatively speaking, his subject matter was mundane, but the crowd stayed with him even through paraphrases of abstruse points from Niebuhr. "And I want to tell you this evening that it is not enough for us to talk about love," he said. "Love is one of the pinnacle parts of the Christian faith. There is another side called justice. And justice is really love in calculation. Justice is love correcting that which would work against love." He said that God was not just the God of love: "He's also the God that standeth before the nations and says, 'Be still and know that I am God—and if you don't obey Me I'm gonna break the backbone of your power—and cast you out of the arms of your international and national relationships.'" Shouts and claps continued at a steady rhythm as King's audacity overflowed. "Standing beside love is always justice," he said. "Not only are we using the tools of persuasion—but we've got to use the tools of coercion." He called again for unity. For working together. He appealed to history, summoning his listeners to behave so that sages of the future would look back at the Negroes of Montgomery and say they were "a people who had the moral courage to stand up for their rights." He said they could do that. "God grant that we will do it before it's too late." Someone said, "Oh, yes." And King said, "As we proceed with our program—let us think on these things."

The crowd retreated into stunned silence as he stepped away from the pulpit. The ending was so abrupt, so anticlimactic. The crowd had been waiting for him to reach for the heights a third time at this conclusion, following the rules of oratory. A few seconds passed before memory and spirit overtook disappointment. The applause continued as King made his way out of the church, with people reaching out to touch him. Dexter members marveled, having never seen King let loose like that. [Ralph] Abernathy remained behind, reading negotiating demands from the pulpit. The boycott was on. King would work on his timing, but his oratory had just made him forever a public person. In the few short minutes of his first political address, a power of communion emerged from him that would speak inexorably to strangers who would both love and revile him, like all prophets. He was twenty-six, and had not quite twelve years and four months to live.

7

Blinded by Might
The Problem with Heaven on Earth

CAL THOMAS AND ED DOBSON

HEAVEN ON EARTH has been a false assumption promised and practiced for centuries by people who forget about the separation that took place in the Garden of Eden after our first parents sinned by trying to be "like God."

Since then, numerous attempts have been made to repair or improve the lives and societies of flawed people. All have failed, though certainly some improvements in combating man's lower nature can be recognized—child labor laws, civil rights for some Americans, though not for unborn Americans—because such efforts have not taken into account the nature of man (sinful) and the folly of sinful man trying to reform himself through institutions.

In the first part of the twentieth century, the Prohibition movement sought to create a "trickle-down morality" effect by legislating against alcohol, as if that substance, not irresponsible behavior, were to blame for negative social conditions. Prohibition was a noble attempt to cure a problem that was rooted not in a bottle but in the soul. It failed because churches relied more on government than on the power of their life-changing message.

In the latter part of this century, the Moral Majority and the Christian Coalition also tried to change society from the top. Their view, always implicit, sometimes explicit, was that rearranging politicians and judges could significantly alter the way sinful man believed and acted. They failed because the problem that produced the social conditions was internal, not external.

In our book *Blinded by Might: Can the Religious Right Save America?*, we affirm the right and responsibility of every person, religious or not, to participate in the political process. But we warn that when the clergy and other institutions of the church do so, they run the risk of being compromised and their central message obscured as they are often seduced by the siren song of temporal political power. It is never the state that is threatened, as liberal clergy and secularists have claimed. It is always the church that suffers, because the kingdom of no compromise that the church is supposed to represent becomes involved in a political kingdom that is all about compromise and almost always is seduced by the world and follows its appeals and agendas, rather than leading the world to the only agenda that can change a life: Jesus Christ.

As just one example of how politics can corrupt the church, or at least those who presume to speak for God, we cite a *New York Times* report in August 1999 in which two former members of the Christian Coalition described that organization's tactics. According to the two, the Christian Coalition lied about the number of its members, counting dead people, double counting others, and adding to their membership list anyone who so much as called with a question. The two also reported that when the organization knew that news crews were to visit, it hired temporary workers to fool the media into believing it was larger and had a greater impact than it actually did.

Are these the tactics most people would associate with someone, or some organization, that uses the name "Christian" as part of its title? If conservative Christians really want to affect their world, they already possess the power to do so. It is the power that Paul referred to in Colossians 1:27: "Christ in you." This is not a call for retreat or disengagement, as some have falsely claimed about our book. It is about an engagement that has more power with greater potential for results than the false promise of politics. Consider the Republican congressional class of 1994, the one that rode to majority power on a wave of "family values." Former speaker Newt Gingrich is divorcing his second wife. Affairs and divorces among several

other conservative Republican members of the Senate and House have also
been reported. If people who ran on "family values" cannot even impose
them on themselves, what makes us think they will be more successful
imposing them on the country through the legislative process?

Conservative Christians seem to think that having their people legis-
late and adjudicate will force those who disagree to accept their views. But
how many of them have accepted Bill Clinton's views since he's been in
office? In politics, if our side wins the next election, the other side does not
acquiesce to the truth of our side's ideas. It simply fights harder to defeat
our side in the election after that. Truth is never advanced.

The Bible that conservative Christians love to wave—rhetorically and
physically—speaks of a world that is passing away and commands us, "Do
not love the world or anything in the world. If anyone loves the world, the
love of the Father is not in him. For everything in the world—the cravings
of sinful man, the lust of his eyes and the boasting of what he has and
does—comes not from the Father but from the world. The world and its
desires pass away, but the man who does the will of God lives forever" (1
John 2:15-17).

Does this mean conservative Christians should retreat into separatism
and a catacomb-like existence? No. Believers should engage the world. They
should just not marry it. Nowhere in Scripture are believers commanded
to "reclaim culture," or "reclaim America." Quite the opposite. C. S. Lewis
has noted that Jesus viewed such things, not as unimportant but as trivial
to his ultimate mission, which was not the reform of nations but the transformation of individuals. The Jewish prophet Isaiah said God views all
nations, presumably including the United States, as "a drop in the bucket."

Christians can and should vote. They can and should also do what
Jesus commanded them to do: feed the hungry, clothe the naked, visit those
in prison, and care for widows and orphans. In doing such things they
make their faith attractive to unbelievers. But they win no converts when
they seek to use the temporal power of government, alone, to impose their
views from the top down. In fact they are doomed to frustration because
there are not enough of them who all believe the same things. In 1996, exit
polls indicated that one-third of the self-described "Evangelical vote" (which
is a minority, not a majority) went to Bill Clinton.

The problem for religiously conservative institutions is that obedience to the commands of Jesus won't raise money, at least not the kinds of money needed to convey the illusion of power and success. Fundraisers have told us they can't raise money on positive themes, so passions must be inflamed and fears enhanced. That's why abortion, homosexuality, and gun control remain the bread and butter fundraising issues for the so-called religious right. Money is raised, but the stated goals are never achieved, nor can they be, because they proceed from the wrong premise and use tactics (sometimes dishonest) in the name of God that He refuses to honor.

The response to our book has been fascinating. From religious leaders who are advocating increased political activism, the reaction has been largely negative. They have accused us of promoting the complete withdrawal of Christians from the political arena even though we repeatedly remind Christians of their responsibility to Caesar. It makes us wonder if they have read the entire book. They have also accused us of saying that all the efforts of Christians for the past twenty years have been a complete waste of time. This is not what we said or believe. The Moral Majority has made two major contributions to the political arena. First, it registered millions of new voters. Second, it forced public discussion on moral issues, such as abortion. Did it accomplish all it set out to do? No. Was it a complete failure? No. We have been most disappointed that those who have reacted negatively to the book have not dealt with the biblical and theological issues that we raised in discussing the relationship between the church, the family, and the state.

The reaction of pastors, however, has been overwhelmingly positive. Most pastors we know struggle with finding the biblical balance in dealing with moral issues and how they relate to the political arena. They are under constant pressure from national organizations as well as people in their own churches to be more politically engaged and active. This pressure is hard to resist, and if they are hesitant they are accused of being weak on the moral issues. They are told that they are what is wrong with America. These pastors appreciate the stand we take in the book and are telling us so.

Our goal for our book was not to have the final word. We acknowledge that we could be wrong in some areas, but if the Bible is to be our guide in some things (such as the way to God, human relationships, justice, and caring about the poor), then it must also be a guide in other, indeed all things, such as the relationship to the state by members of an eternal kingdom whose head is a king that never stands for election.

Both the religious left and religious right go wrong when their theologies and practices are selective. They take from God those things that seem to bless their political agendas and reject or ignore those things that won't raise money or that make them feel uncomfortable. God doesn't offer us any choice, except to reject Him. He requires that if we are to know Him and serve Him with His approval, we must accept the entire package, not just the ribbon or the wrapping. That both left and right have failed to do this is the primary reason why neither has been effective in serving the church or having a positive and long-lasting impact on the state.

8

Progressive Politics and Visions
and, Uh, Well . . . God

RICHARD PARKER

WHAT DOES COME to mind when someone mentions "American religion" nowadays? Aren't Jerry Falwell, Pat Robertson, Gary Bauer, or antiabortion or antigay picketers probably the first images? Or is it perhaps Bill Clinton, lachrymose at a Washington prayer breakfast last year, earnestly "repenting" his affair with Monica?

More recently what about the House Republicans voting that schools post the Ten Commandments as the answer to gun violence? Or the discomforting sudden embrace of religion by this year's crop of presidential candidates and their minions?

It's not a list designed to warm most progressive hearts. Nor should it.

Yet it's far from all we need to know or care about American religion. Contrary to what many may think, not only is religion alive and well in America, but it's growing in scope and influence today—and a good deal of what it says and does is progressive.

Of course, religion has always been present in America's life. John Winthrop's "City on the Hill" provides a starting point, and Tocqueville reports on its centrality to civic life and politics 200 years later. Even Marx saw we were different. "America," he wrote, "is pre-eminently the country of religiosity, as Beaumont, Tocqueville and the Englishman Hamilton unanimously assure us. . . . We find that [American] religion not only exists, but displays a *fresh and vigorous vitality*."[1]

No one who reflects even for a moment on abolition, suffrage, temperance, various utopian and reform movements, or the Progressive Era—or more recently, on civil rights, the Vietnam era, and the 1980s battles over Central America or nuclear weapons—can miss the vital role of religious leaders, religious visions, or religious communities in any of these transformative struggles.

But what about today?

Here's what surprises a lot of my liberal friends: in Los Angeles, you'll find that progressive religious tradition alive in CLUE, a broad-based coalition of ministers, priests, and rabbis, that was at the heart of the city's successful Living Wage campaign last year. In Boston, it's in the Greater Boston Interfaith Organization (GBIO), a new ecumenical social justice organization working on local job creation and school reforms. At its founding meeting, nearly 5,000 people heard religious leaders from Cardinal Law to inner-city black Pentecostal ministers and suburban Unitarians and Episcopalians preaching a new era of faith-led urban renewal.

In Washington, a liberal evangelical group called Sojourners regularly challenges its conservative brethren on issues from their stances on women and race to economic inequality and support for organized labor. Sojourners, to the surprise of skeptics, is drawing increasing attention and influence among America's largest bloc of white Christians, many of whom seem to be increasingly uncomfortable with the "Christian right" legacy of the 1980s and early 1990s. A few blocks away, coordinators for the religious alliance Jubilee 2000 are pressing Congress to abolish the foreign debts of the world's poorest countries, drawing on the Old Testament example of "the Jubilee Year" when debtors were to be forgiven their debts, and slaves set free.

In New York, meanwhile, working out of offices at the Cathedral of St. John the Divine, a new religiously based environmental group called the National Religious Partnership for the Environment (with the help of $10 million from Pew, MacArthur, and other foundations) is pressing churches to take up global warming, toxic pollution controls, Brazilian rainforests, and ecological sustainability as part of their everyday ministry. Not far away, over in East Brooklyn, a group of mostly black and Hispanic activist ministers and laypeople, calling themselves the Nehemiah Project, is putting the finishing touches on the latest round of nearly 5,000 units of low-income housing it has built or rehabilitated in the past fifteen years.[2]

Along the southeastern seaboard, stretching from Delaware to Georgia, faith-based groups are working to organize thousands of mainly black and female workers in the enormous low-wage poultry-processing industry. Down in Texas, the Industrial Areas Foundation has, with religious funding and religious support, been building effective ecumenical, faith-based grassroots coalitions among lower-income black and Hispanic communities for two decades that have campaigned for housing, jobs, education, and community investment.

Unknown to most of my progressive friends, America's Catholic bishops, mainly through their Campaign for Human Development, meanwhile regularly contribute $10–$20 million a year to grassroots progressive groups around the country, working on everything from inner-city community renewal in Chicago, to tenant organizing in California, to minority issues in more than a dozen states. And millions more flow each year from Catholic orders like the Maryknolls and Jesuits, as well as mainline Protestant denominations and liberal Jewish groups.

In short, there's a great deal going on in America's religious life that too many of America's liberals and progressives should know more about—and support. Yet the fact is we often do neither.

Gary Wills thinks that our ignorance—and the ignorance of liberals and intellectuals—about American religion reflects a deeper blindness about America. In *Under God*, he's blunt about his views:

> The learned have their superstitions, prominent among them a belief that superstition is evaporating. . . . Every time religiosity catches the attention of intellectuals, it is as if a shooting star has appeared in the sky. One could hardly guess, from this, that nothing has been more stable in our history, nothing less budgeable, than religious belief and practice.[3]

The charge has a decided edge to it, but if you look at nearly a half century of polling data about Americans and religion, it's not hard to see why Wills feels the way he does. According to Gallup, for example,

—Nine out of ten Americans say they've never doubted the existence of God;

—Eight out of ten Americans believe they'll be called before God on Judgment Day to answer for their sins;

—Seven in ten say they are current church, synagogue, or mosque members;

—Four in ten say they worship at least weekly (six in ten say at least monthly) as members of a religious congregation.[4]

All this cuts against the confident belief once held that religion, whatever its past history, was in terminal decline—thanks to the "secularizing" forces of urbanization, industrialization, scientific explanation, and consumer culture. In Britain, France, and Germany, for example, barely more than a tenth of citizens say they worship weekly, with those who say they believe in God hovering between a quarter and third—both small fractions of the comparable U.S. figures.[5]

Teasing out—and debating—the reasons for this "American exceptionalism" is a cottage industry among social scientists who study religion. What's perhaps more important on the eve of a new century is the simple fact of American religion's durability—and its implications for progressive politics in the decades ahead.

The first overwhelming fact about American religion is this: nearly 60 percent of Americans identify themselves as Protestants, 25 percent as Catholic, 2 percent each as Jews or Mormons, about 1 percent as Orthodox Christians, another 1 or 2 percent as "other religions" (mostly Muslim, Buddhist, or Hindu). Barely a tenth of Americans say they have no religious identity.[6]

At first glance, of course, those numbers alone make America an overwhelmingly "Christian" country—more Christian, in fact, than India is Hindu, Israel is Jewish, or Latin America is Catholic. That 85 percent "Christian majority," however, is—and always has been—deeply and fractiously divided. For example, between 1,200 and 1,500 different denominations parse Protestantism's 150 million members into often wafer-thin subgroupings.[7]

As a consequence, more relevant dividing lines turn on denominational identity and their rough "family" location. Another way to look at that immense Christian bloc, for example, is this: about a quarter of Americans are Catholic, a quarter mainline Protestant, a quarter Fundamentalist Protestant, and a tenth black Protestants.

The lines between those "family" groupings aren't just ceremonial or superficial. To the contrary, they're powerful and real—and have long influenced not just religious boundaries but political and social beliefs. Catholics, for example, from their initial large-scale migration in the 1830s right up to the 1960s, found themselves isolated in a sea of Protestant ire and suspicion that imparted a distinctive pattern to their political allegiances. Protestant Fundamentalists, meanwhile, heavily concentrated in the South, placed themselves at odds with their northern and midwestern brethren even before the Civil War, not only over slavery but intractable issues involving the inerrancy of the Bible—and later the role of science.

Black Protestants—black Americans were, and are, overwhelmingly Protestant—when faced with the nation's enduring racism and religious isolation, constructed their own distinctive faith culture and denominations, blending the spiritualism and directness of the Fundamentalists with the more liberal social and political attitudes of the Mainliners' leadership. And no American Jew doubts the important divides among the Reform, Conservative, Reconstructionist, Orthodox and ultra-Orthodox, or the echoes even today of once-powerful divisions between German and East European immigrant traditions.

Despite all our talk about "postmodernism," at the end of the twentieth century those old divisions still carry measurable effects. For example, Catholics are second only to Jews as a group in deeply distrusting both TV evangelists and the Christian right—two groups in turn almost uniformly drawn from the ranks of Protestant Fundamentalists. Even among the Protestant majority, there are sharp differences: Mainliners as a group are much less likely to watch TV evangelists or support the Christian right than are Fundamentalists.

On a polarizing issue like abortion, similarly distinct divisions occur: 60 percent of Fundamentalist Protestants say they oppose abortion in virtually all circumstances, versus 41 percent of Catholics, 23 percent of mainline Protestants, and 3 percent of Jews. On the issue of public funding of private schools—central to the hotly debated "voucher" issue nowadays, 45 percent of Fundamentalists support it, as do 58 percent of Catholics, but only 34 percent of Mainliners and 24 percent of Jews.[8]

Across a wide range of public issues, similar distinctions obtain: whether it's peace, the environment, civil rights, support for unions, and so on, simple grouping by these large religious "blocs" or by denominations produces variations in support or opposition that can range from 10 percent to 30 percent, even 40 percent, depending on the issue.

You can see these large fault lines in the denominations' social teaching as clearly as in the poll results.

The large mainline Protestant "family," for example, is generally doctrinally "progressive" on a wide variety of social and political issues. Here is an excerpt from the foundational "Social Principles" of the United Methodist Church:

> We claim all economic systems to be under the judgment of God no less than other facets of the created order. Therefore, we recognize the responsibility of governments to develop and implement sound fiscal and monetary policies that provide for the economic life [of] individuals and corporate entities, and that ensure full employment and adequate incomes with a minimum of inflation. We believe private and public enterprises are responsible for the social costs of doing business, such as employment and environment pollution, and that they should be held accountable for these costs. We support measures that would reduce the concentration of wealth in the hands of a few. We further support efforts to revise tax structures and eliminate governmental support that now benefit the wealthy at the expense of other persons.[9]

The Methodists go on to call for limiting the rights of private property, upholding collective bargaining, the advancement of more meaningful work and leisure, an end to celebration of consumerism, and immediate action against world poverty, as well as calling for specific measures to help migrant labor, limit gambling, break up corporate monopolies, and increase various forms of "work sharing" and decentralized management on the job.

Even a cursory reading of this and similar Methodist resolutions indicates that the Methodists' vision is much more progressive than anything emanating from Democratic Party platforms or policies in the past thirty years—and represents claims that are meant to serve as core social teachings for more than 10 million Americans.[10]

Or consider recent formal statements by the Presbyterian Church U.S.A. to its 4 million members that demand "nothing less than a full-scale assault on poverty at home and abroad, endorsing the provision of national health care, increases in the minimum wage and job-training programs, more investment in housing and education, an increase in U.S. international aid, and the development of a comprehensive plan to revive city life in the United States."[11]

Presbyterians then went on—in the midst of the Republicans' Contract with America and President Clinton's cynical embrace of "triangulation" to explicitly condemn the "large amount of negative campaigning, neglect of the worthiness of the political vocation, and . . . the undue influence [of moneyed interests] in the election process," and called for local Presbyterian clergy to speak out on behalf of "our historical commitment to working for economic justice, peace and disarmament, racial and civil rights."[12]

The 2.5-million-member Episcopal Church is as explicitly unconservative as its larger Methodist and Presbyterian brethren—in some cases even more so. Its most recent national convention, for example, condemned Clinton's welfare reforms, urged new public support for migrant laborers, pressed for strict gun control and the abolition of nuclear weapons, and for a new trial for Philadelphia death-row prisoner Mumia Abu-Jamal. It also committed the church to supporting local "living wage" campaigns and launched a comprehensive study of "the theology of work" to begin redressing not only the material, but moral and civic, inequalities that have emerged in the past three decades.

The Catholic Church—its stance on gender and abortion notwithstanding—is no less progressive than these mainline Protestant denominations on a host of social and political issues that progressives count as important. The U.S. bishops pastoral letter "Economic Justice for All," written in the 1980s, for example, is still a benchmark statement. More recently, in the debate over Clinton's welfare reforms, the Catholic Church was by far the leader among religious groups that openly fought its passage.

These broadly shared progressive positions of the Catholics, Methodists, Presbyterians, and Episcopalians are moreover shared by the United Church of Christ, American Baptists, Evangelical Lutherans, several black Baptist and Methodist denominations, as well as the smaller Unitarians and Quakers.

Taken together, the mainline Protestants form the cornerstone of the 52-million-member National Council of Churches, for fifty years the institutional forum for progressive and liberal Protestantism in the United States (and bête noire of groups like the Christian Coalition). The Catholic Church, meanwhile, can lay claim to nearly 60 million members alone, while the mostly politically progressive black Protestant churches count 20-million-plus Americans and Jewish organizations several million more.

Unlike untold numbers of political "causes" and "movements" that have arisen and then disappeared, these large denominations aren't going away. Moreover, many of them have been active pillars of progressive public policy throughout much of the twentieth century, and steadfastly (even increasingly) so since Vietnam and the civil rights era. In the 1970s, these were religious communities that actively sought greater equality for women, endorsed a new environmental worldview, and in the 1980s were often vocal opponents of Ronald Reagan's policies at home and abroad.

Yet the most intriguing feature today about this entire progressive tradition in American religion, and its history, is its invisibility to those not part of it. The reasons for that "invisibility" aren't always easy to disentangle. Partly it has had to do with the secularization of the nation's elites in both the universities and the press. As a group, these Americans have been uncomfortable with and distrustful of religion generally—and draw on both Enlightenment and modern liberalism's suspicions about religion's historical tendency to generate intolerance and bloodshed as reasons for its rejection. One study of the elite Washington press corps, for example, found that 86 percent seldom or never attended religious services.[13]

Equally important has been the redrawing of the important "identity" maps in American life, especially since the 1960s. Religious affiliation (in particular, denomination) once served as a distinctive marker of one's location in America's social structure, as evidenced by a thriving social science literature on denomination and social class—most famously, H. Richard Niebuhr's *Social Sources of Denominationalism*.[14]

After World War II, a new spirit of ecumenism and the softening of denominational and religious borders—most celebrated in Will Heberg's 1950s classic *Protestant, Catholic, Jew*—set the stage for what Sydney

Ahlstrom, in his Pulitzer-prize-winning history of American religion, called the "coming of post-Protestant America."[15] Particularly since the 1960s, gender, race, and sexual preference has taken on new defining importance—and powerfully submerged the older coordinates of religion, ethnicity, region, and class. Redressing the inequalities associated with those ascendent categories, needless to say, became in no small part the defining mission of liberals and progressives alike.

At the same time, the 1960s also marked the beginning of a decline in religious membership (compared at least with the decades immediately prior) and in the prestige of religious institutions—part of a decline of confidence and participation in civil society more generally. Nowhere was this decline felt more powerfully than among the mainline Protestants, Methodists, and Presbyterians particularly. Catholicism suffered its own declines among Americans of European descent but compensated with a dramatic inflow of Hispanic members, while Jews—who have dropped from 4 percent to 2 percent of Americans in the past fifty years (and have lost significant portions of their religiously active population)—arguably have sought new symbolic self-identification in part through images of both Israel and the Holocaust.

Although the 1990s saw a partial reversal of those trends, the public rise first of Jerry Falwell and his Moral Majority in the late 1970s—and then (as the Moral Majority faced bankruptcy) of Pat Robertson and the Christian Coalition—seemed to firmly establish conservative Fundamentalist Protestants as the new religious ascendancy.

In their fascination with the Christian right, many liberals have openly wondered why religious progressives haven't created their own liberal "Christian Coalitions"—a fair question on its face, but in fact one that both misreads what the Christian right has (and hasn't) accomplished and ignores profound differences in the nature of religiosity and organizational structure between the liberal and conservative tradtions.

Whether progressive denominations could or want to "replicate" the Christian right's overt intervention in the electoral process is an open question. First, these faiths—particularly the mainline Protestants—draw on much different approaches to religion, which emphasize a more cerebral, less visceral embrace of faith. Belief in biblical inerrancy, the emotional reality of imminent salvation and the perils of damnation, the evangelical demand to save souls one by one, and the deep-seated suspicion of science and other powerful institutions that compete with religion for authority—all these are generally alien to mainline, and in somewhat different ways Catholic, belief.

Second, the Christian right isn't a denomination but rather a network of nonprofit groups that draws money and members from mainly conservative Fundamentalist Protestant denominations and free-standing congregations. Why the progressive religious community hasn't built its own competitor to the Christian Coalition, though, is a question partly answered by the difficulties in finding common voice among mainline Protestants, Catholics, and Jews, as well as the fact that religiously progressive individuals already have plenty of opportunities to engage the electoral system.

Comparative studies of mainliners, Catholics, Jews, and Fundamentalists find dramatic differences in the kinds and levels of involvement by their members in other, nonreligious, civic and political organizations. mainline Protestants and Jews, for example, (as sociologist Robert Wuthnow and other repeatedly find) are much more likely than Fundamentalists to donate to a party, speak publicly, serve in some public leadership role, or belong to civically engaged (and more liberal) nonprofit groups—by a margin of two to one or more.[16]

There's a second issue here about "replicating" the religious right. Recent research by a number of scholars and pollsters, for example, has suggested a more cautionary reading of the Christian right's successes. As several political scientists have found, rather than actually generating a dramatic rise in the number of adherents (as it claims), more accurately the Christian right found itself riding the Republican realignment of traditionally conservative Southern voters—a process initiated by the civil rights stance of Lyndon Johnson and Martin Luther King, Jr., not the organizing abilities of Falwell or Robertson.

In the midst of this realignment, the Christian right certainly helped crystallize the alienation and resentment of many conservatives–which had peaked in the wake of "the Sixties"—but even this is more uncertain than it may appear. In some studies, despite reams of news coverage, as few as one in ten Americans claimed to know much about the Christian right, while an equally small number actively identified themselves with the movement. Even among Fundamentalists, Gallup found that more claimed *not to know* about the Moral Majority than supported it (38 percent versus 36 percent).[17] And despite repeated attempts by both the Christian Coalition and Moral Majority to "reach out" beyond their base within Protestant Fundamentalism to conservative Catholics, mainline Protestants, and Jews, the efforts proved dismally unsuccessful. In 1997, after Ralph Reed left and the coalition faced layoffs and budget cuts, for example, the first project closed was their "outreach" program to conservative Catholics.

People can reasonably disagree about whether the whole Christian right phenomenon has peaked and is in decline—or has merely gone "underground" to focus on state and local politics, as some believe. Significantly, though, both Paul Weyrich Jr. and Cal Thomas—major figures in the movement—now argue that the time has come for Fundamentalists to turn away from electoral politics and focus on traditional evangelical concerns.[18]

Meanwhile, America's progressive religious community goes on—for the most part ignored by those who like to think of themselves as progressive but who have no connection to the nation's religious world. Of course, one can't count all the members or leaders of these churches and synagogues as avid supporters of their denominations' official views—like the Democratic Party or labor unions, large blocs of progressive religion's constituencies find themselves indifferent, even hostile, to the voices of their leaders.

Yet the central fact remains: in an era when progressive voices seem few in number, when many progressive organizations struggle to meet payrolls, let alone advance agendas, there is a large body of committed, enduring, and caring human beings—deeply bound, out of their own understanding of the connection between justice and the divine—who seek a world most of us could generously affirm.

Built on values untested by the latest polls, sensitive to their constituents but ever mindful that they are called to witness for more than immediate or personal advantage, they struggle with their own limitations, their own internal conflicts and weaknesses—and yet have emerged time and again over American history, resistant to the abuses of the human family, willing to fight for a world beyond this parsimonious age of ours.

9

Learning from Nehemiah

KURT L. SCHMOKE

Twenty-five years ago, when I was a student at Harvard Law School, an African Methodist Episcopal pastor in Cambridge, Massachusetts, the Reverend John Bryant, called a group of us law students together. His message to us that day was straightforward. He urged us to become "modern-day Nehemiahs."

He was referring, of course, to the Old Testament prophet. Chapter 2, verses 17 and 18 of the Book of Nehemiah describes Nehemiah returning to his hometown of Jerusalem and finding it in ruins. "Ye see the distress that we are in, how Jerusalem lieth waste," he tells his friends and neighbors. He calls on them, "Come and let us build the wall of Jerusalem, that we be no more a reproach." Nehemiah assures the ancient Hebrews that he speaks with God's blessing. He tells them of "the hand of my God which was good upon me." His friends and neighbors heed his words, responding, "Let us rise up and build." And so, we learn, "they strengthened their hands for this good work."

Brick by brick, beam by beam, section by section, the people of Jerusalem rebuilt the walls of the city. And in the process they were healed and empowered, and hope was restored to their community.

I'm not a preacher-politician. My typical speeches could never be mistaken for sermons. But the bedrock principle behind much of my work as mayor of the city of Baltimore can be found in that biblical story. As was the ancient city of Jerusalem, Baltimore, in part an urban gem, is scarred by distress and waste that take many forms. Substance abuse. Crime and violence. AIDS. Dilapidated housing. Inadequate health care. Underfunded schools. Unemployment and underemployment. Neglected children. It's a long and depressing litany.

But in the spirit of the Nehemiah Principle, Baltimore has seen people coming together—people from government, the private sector, and nonprofit organizations, especially the faith community—to erase the signs of distress and waste and build a brighter future for our community, just as the people of Jerusalem did for their community so many centuries ago. In three areas in particular we have put the Nehemiah Principle into practice. The first is housing, the second is substance abuse, the third is early childhood education.

BUILD—Baltimoreans United in Leadership Development—is a multiracial, ecumenical, citywide organization comprising forty-five churches, one union (a local affiliate of the American Federation of State, County, and Municipal Employees), and four neighborhood associations. During my first campaign for mayor in 1987, members of BUILD approached me asking to work in partnership with the residents of one of our most impoverished neighborhoods—a place called Sandtown-Winchester—to rebuild that community

Not long after I was elected, I traveled with members of BUILD to see a housing development program in Brooklyn, New York, sponsored by the Interfaith Church, one of BUILD's sister institutions. I also traveled to Israel—appropriately enough, to Jerusalem—to see a community development initiative there.

These experiences helped shape the comprehensive, community-driven effort to revitalize Sandtown-Winchester that continues today. The centerpiece of that effort is new housing. Much of the funding comes through a federal grant called, yes, Nehemiah. The remainder comes from city, state, and private sources. BUILD itself raised some $2.2 million toward the initial construction and rehabilitation of 300 Nehemiah Homes in Sandtown and a neighboring community and another 27 in another impoverished area of the city called Cherry Hill. BUILD went into the community. BUILD talked about rebuilding the area. And then BUILD did it.

The citizens themselves planned it, and together with BUILD and the clergy they began to turn their community around. What once looked like a bombed-out area now looks far more like a neighborhood of choice. At times it was hard to know what was going up faster—the new housing or the number of church-related 501(c)(3) nonprofit organizations. The clergy would come to us and say they had an idea. We would say, "That's great." Then we would look at the government's regulations. To get around them, we would ask if Trinity Baptist could simply become Trinity Development, Inc. In the process of filing the papers, by the way, I found out that a lot of deacons like to be the presidents of corporations.

Today, Sandtown-Winchester remains a work in progress, with hurdles still to be overcome and dreams still to be fulfilled. But already it has drawn the attention of many of the nation's top political and urban leaders and has sparked similar attempts at community revitalization in other U.S. cities.

Thanks to our church leaders, we have also had some success in the area of drugs. In Baltimore we have a daunting problem with drugs. We estimate that our city is home to 59,000 heroin and cocaine addicts. Now, understand what that means. If you assume that all those people are over the age of eighteen, that means that one in eight of the adult citizens of Baltimore has a serious substance-abuse problem.

Obviously, we cannot incarcerate our way out of that problem. Many different strategies are needed to control what I see as a three-headed monster—because the so-called drug problem involves the problem of crime, the problem of addiction, and the problem of AIDS. At least two of the three are health problems primarily, not criminal justice problems, and thus require not a criminal justice war but a public health war—one that looks at most of the abusers out there as patients to be treated rather than criminals to be incarcerated.

What to do? I went to the pastors. I told them how serious the AIDS problem was in Baltimore. All around the country AIDS rates are going down. Yet in Baltimore the AIDS rates have been steadily creeping up— mostly because of the intravenous drug users sharing dirty needles with people and having sex with innocent partners, resulting, most horribly, in babies being born with AIDS.

I told the pastors that we had to do something that they might not like. We had to start a sterile syringe exchange program to get clean needles out on the street. Now, you can imagine that the first time I approached the clergy with that idea, a few people wanted me *under* the church. But we talked it through, and some of our clergy leaders told us about the many funerals they had preached and the way families had been affected. Before long the clergy became the primary advocates for the needle exchange program. They went down to the legislature and became a simply irresistible force. I had lobbied the legislature myself for three years with no results. What turned the tide was an enormous outpouring from the Interdenominational Ministerial Alliance. Leaders of more than 150 churches, synagogues, and mosques asked the legislature for a chance to try our idea. Give us at least a pilot program, they said. See whether it works. We believe it is important, and we will back it.

Their request was granted. We started the program, and after the third year a study by the Johns Hopkins School of Public Health showed a huge decrease in the transmission of HIV in Baltimore. When the legislature passed the legislation the first time in 1994, the margin of victory was one vote. When we went back to get it renewed four years later, all but one legislator in the state voted for it. That was a dramatic change—though not as dramatic as the change the program has meant for our city. And it would never have happened without the leadership of the faith-based organizations.

Finally, our after-school programs. When you think about those 59,000 drug addicts, and you start multiplying that number by families and neighborhoods, you can see that a huge number of children will be affected by this substance abuse problem if we just let them out of school at three o'clock and send them back to their neighborhoods.

We wanted to offer some after-school options for these children, but we could not figure out how to do it. Then in 1996 members of BUILD came to us and said they would like to create something called the Child First Authority. They wanted to help raise money to supplement public schools and offer after-school programs in a number of schools to protect children from being victims of crime at their time of greatest risk—between the hours of three and six in the afternoon. Under pressure from

BUILD, the state agreed to add funding to Baltimore's start-up money. A number of private donors stepped in, too, including Baltimore Orioles owner Peter Angelos. Today, Child First Authority operates after-school programs in ten Baltimore city schools, serving more than 1,200 children. Eventually BUILD hopes to offer these programs in as many as forty schools.

But the faith-based organizations in Baltimore didn't stop there. They knew that in the mornings before school and the afternoons after school, a lot of children have to go through very rough neighborhoods. To help those children, the churches in these areas put little signs up in their windows. The signs featured a steeple and a little smiley face, and at the bottom were the words: Safe Haven. If a child walking to school felt threatened, he or she could go into that church and know there would be a caring adult there, whether it was the pastor or someone else. Somebody was going to be there. As with the Child First Authority, the Safe Haven programs have increased school attendance dramatically in some of Baltimore's hard-pressed neighborhoods.

In all three of these areas, the faith community, the clergy leaders in particular, have joined in and carried out the vision of Nehemiah. "Yes," they have said, in typical Old Testament style. "Let us rise up and build."

What is happening in Baltimore exemplifies a growing trend that bodes well for the future of our cities. All over the nation, faith-based organizations are joining with government and the residents of our most blighted urban neighborhoods to help renew these communities—spiritually, physically, economically. To witness these efforts is to see the Nehemiah Principle in action—and to strengthen one's own faith in God's essential goodness.

10

Having Faith in Our Neighborhoods
The Front Porch Alliance

STEPHEN GOLDSMITH

THE SCENE ON Indianapolis's east side seemed almost symbolic. On one side of the street was Shepherd Community Ministries, a center that served vulnerable and disadvantaged families. On the other side was a narrow alley where crack deals were made on a regular basis. It was as though the forces of good and evil were facing off across Washington Street.

Shepherd's director, Pastor Jay Height, was tired of worrying that the children he worked with every day might wind up on the wrong side of the street. So he came up with an idea: turn the crack alley into a park, a well-lit green area that drug dealers would shun. There was only one problem. To have the alley vacated, he would have to work with more than fifty separate contacts—agencies within city government, neighborhood organizations, utilities, assessors, and others.

Most people would have thrown up their hands and walked away. Instead, Pastor Height contacted the Front Porch Alliance (FPA), a city agency that works with value-shaping organizations, particularly faith-based organizations. Because the FPA employees understood how city procedures worked, they could help Pastor Height vacate the alley. "Granted, it is not always as successful as you would like, but in this case, we were able to make it work through teamwork," said Pastor Height, "And the neat thing to me is to be able to look at it and say, "Here is something beautiful."

Once the FPA cleared away government obstacles, many concerned organizations sprang forward to help make the neighborhood safer. Keep Indianapolis Beautiful, a private nonprofit group, designed the new park and supervised its construction. The two businesses that adjoined the old alley agreed to become the park's nominal owners. Volunteers from Youth for Christ put down soil and planted flowers.

This raises some important questions about why and how much government should get involved in troubled neighborhoods. Suppose you told Pastor Height's story to two political theorists, one traditionally conservative, the other traditionally liberal. The conservative would nod knowingly and explain that once cumbersome government regulations were out of the way, the neighborhood improved on its own. "Not at all," the liberal would retort. "The alley couldn't have been vacated if government hadn't become actively involved."

The director of the FPA, Isaac Randolph, puts it another way. "Everyone agrees that government has a core responsibility," he says. "But the core has a circumference, and the controversy is over the size of the circumference. Conservatives use a microscope to measure it; liberals use a yardstick." In Indianapolis, we have realized that neither approach is right. The traditional liberal belief in massive governmental intervention is misguided, but so is the idea that government should abandon neighborhoods altogether. There is a role for government to play in neighborhood revitalization. But what is it, if it is not the oversized federal programs that plague our cities today?

Indianapolis's experience of outsourcing municipal services may provide a useful comparison. Although we have attracted national attention for privatizing services, it wasn't simply privatization that allowed us to save over $420 million. Rather, it was competition between government agencies and private companies: whoever offered to do the best job at the lowest cost won the contract. In other words, it didn't matter whether municipal services were performed by the government or by the private sector; what mattered was that government outsourced those services fairly, supervised them closely, and made sure they were being provided well.

The same principle, with a few modifications, can be applied to neighborhood revitalization. City government is certainly responsible for urban neighborhoods, just as it is responsible for trash collection, for example. But just because government is responsible for making sure a service is provided doesn't mean that government has to provide that service itself. Just as government can work with private companies to collect trash, it can work with nonprofit organizations to improve neighborhoods.

One job that government can do is simply helping neighborhood organizations understand rules and regulations—especially those for which government itself is responsible. The FPA's part in vacating the crack alley is a good example. Or consider Lakeview Christian Center, a suburban congregation on the west side of Indianapolis. Lakeview had been planning to build another church in the inner city for years, but it was worried about the complicated process of land acquisition. The FPA helped it through the process.

But then the FPA did something else—something even more important. It noticed that one of the city's worst-performing public schools was located near the site of the new church. So the FPA proposed a partnership between Lakeview and the school. Now Lakeview sends tutors to help struggling students, provides food to needy families identified by the school's social worker, and helps run an after-school program for advanced students. The FPA had become what Michael Joyce calls a "civic switchboard," a central body that connects various groups for the public good.

Those two functions—helping neighborhood organizations wade through government rules and acting as a civic switchboard—are comparatively uncontroversial, even when the organizations in question are faith based. The real controversy arises when government begins funding services provided by faith-based organizations. While this controversy isn't surprising, the history of the FPA may show why it is misplaced.

The FPA was founded in 1997, two years into my second term. We had already invested a record $1.35 billion in the city's infrastructure to rebuild the physical structure of neglected inner-city neighborhoods. Then we had turned our attention to an even bigger challenge, strengthening those neighborhoods organizationally. We did that by helping the neighborhoods form umbrella organizations, paying for a full-time neighborhood coordinator for each umbrella, and funding all of them with Community Development Block Grant dollars.

That program was a limited success. We discovered that even though we had budged a little from the traditionally conservative hands-off approach, neighborhoods couldn't provide all the services they needed by themselves. So in 1997 we formed the Front Porch Alliance. We spent months canvassing the city, explaining to community leaders that we wanted to start working with them, supporting them, and even funding them. Once we had a strong base of support in the community, we went public.

The point is that the FPA wasn't intended to include only faith-based organizations. All sorts of value-shaping nonprofits were approached and invited to join us. Some of the organizations had existing specific relationships with city hall, for example, community development corporations worked with (or sometimes against) the Development Department. But as time went on, we discovered that most frequently the new and smaller organizations that chose to become most actively involved in the FPA were faith based.

That wasn't because we were discriminating in favor of faith-based groups. When the Robinson Community African Methodist Episcopal Church decided to open a community center for summer camps, after-school programs, tutoring, and so forth, we leased an abandoned fire station to it cheaply. When the Indianapolis Black Firefighters Association decided to convert another abandoned fire station into a community center, we supported it as well. Our job was to help value-shaping organizations improve their neighborhoods, whether those organizations were faith based or not. Nevertheless, the most frequent and enduring partners surrounded their physical assistance with faith.

Not only should government be sure never to discriminate in favor of religion, it should never force anyone to participate in a religious program. For example, the FPA has initiated a program called Community Involvement, in which youths in the juvenile justice system are referred to faith-based organizations in their neighborhoods. However, the court provides various secular programs as well, which are just as accessible as Community Involvement. No one is assigned to a pastor without choosing that option.

Now let's examine a more difficult question. It makes sense not to discriminate against faith-based organizations when contracting for social services. For instance, when Safe Haven, a foundation that helps victims of domestic violence, needed to find a way to transport children to its programs, we didn't hesitate to set up a partnership with several churches, which were paid to transport the children. But what about hiring faith-based organizations to provide social services that include religious elements? Should government have any part in that?

Many people would say no emphatically—and I think this is a subject about which reasonable people can disagree. However, my view is that so long as government doesn't fund religion directly, it should be able to support social services to which faith-based organizations may add a religious component. That is, if a church runs a homeless shelter with beds paid for by government, it shouldn't be prevented from asking its guests to pray once a day. Again, government should always be sure to support secular shelters as well, so that no one is compelled to enter one with a religious component.

One way to steer clear of some of these issues is to work with nonprofit bodies set up by faith-based organizations. If a church sets up a homeless shelter next door, and if the shelter is an independent 501(c)(3), it is much easier to preserve separation between the church's religious function and the shelter's social service.

Programs like the FPA would be in good shape if the only opposition they faced was from people concerned with the separation of church and state. But we learned the hard way that there was a bigger obstacle: the churches didn't trust us. Faith-based organizations in Indianapolis had long grown accustomed to a negative relationship with government: they were ignored at best and mistreated at worst. When we approached pastors and proposed an alliance, they were highly skeptical. "What's in it for the government?" they kept wondering. "What political hoops do we have to jump through?"

In the end, we secured their support in three ways. First, we established an advisory board and spent time consulting with the organizations and getting their advice before publicly announcing the FPA. This showed them that we wouldn't spring any surprises on them and that we were serious about incorporating their suggestions into our plans. Second, we assisted them immediately and strongly, instead of just talking about it. And third, we invested heavily in the FPA. We tripled its work force from three people to nine—and that's unusual in an administration that has cut the payroll by a quarter. We wanted every pastor who worked with an FPA representative to know that he or she was working with someone who had the mayor's ear.

Once we won over the churches, we faced an even bigger problem—that government employees returned their distrust. Just because my administration formed the FPA didn't mean that every city employee supported the idea. Public employees lacked confidence in the capacity of faith-based organizations. Grant monitors in particular paid closer attention to procedural details—with which the organizations were understandably unfamiliar—than to programs' outcomes. This is still a problem, but the FPA has improved relations by translating between government bureaucracy and informal, good-hearted but not paper-work-minded faith organizations.

Faith-based organizations are a badly underused resource for improving the lives of disadvantaged Americans. As government begins working with them, it will come to realize what we in Indianapolis discovered two years ago: that faith-based organizations are infinitely more capable of handling neighborhood problems than government is. Unlike government officials, faith-based organizations tend to be tied closely to neighborhoods. By working *with* government officials, faith-based organizations can be part of solid solutions.

When I looked out of my window on the twenty-fifth floor of the City-County Building, I saw the whole city, but not any individual neighborhood very well. When a pastor looks out of his window, he sees the people who need help and the houses that need rehabilitation. Sometimes, if he is motivated enough, he even sees the crack alley that needs to be vacated and cleaned up.

But there is another reason that faith-based and value-shaping organizations are such a vital part of our communities. No matter how hard local governments work to keep taxes low, improve municipal services, repair the infrastructure, and so on, true urban strength can only be built on values. Without a population that cares about maintaining a civil society, a city will crumble. Values are best transmitted in two ways, through families and through local value-shaping organizations, particularly faith-based organizations. If government begins to partner with those organizations, they will not only provide services better than government can, they will teach our youth about citizenship, civility, charity, and a host of other values more effectively than ever before.

This is an idea whose time has come. More public servants are beginning to explore the world of possibilities that government-faith partnerships offer. If we succeed—if we encourage organizations like the FPA in cities all over the country, if we promote similar initiatives on a national scale—we will be harnessing the nation's greatest energy to deal with the nation's greatest problems.

PART THREE
Does God Take Sides?

11

Conscience and the Public Square
Heeding the Still, Small Voice

PATRICK GLYNN

DURING 1998—ever to be remembered as the year of the Clinton sex-and-lies scandal—not once did my wife and I hear a reference to Mr. Clinton's troubles from the pulpit of our Catholic church in Olney, Maryland. Our experience in this suburban Catholic parish less than an hour's drive from the nation's capital provided an interesting prism through which to view the relation of religion to politics in America. The attitudes toward politics and religion among the priests and the people at St. Peter's seemed different from, and perhaps healthier than, the views so prevalent in the national debate.

Of course, many ministers and priests across the country, even some Catholic ones, delivered sermons on the Clinton matter. At one point, Cardinal John O'Connor of New York uttered critical words on the president's conduct from the pulpit of St. Patrick's Cathedral. Washington's Cardinal James Hickey was more oblique. In one of his monthly letters to his flock, he pictured "sin" as having "hired an unscrupulous public relations firm to improve its image," employing clever public spokesmen and "the wizardry of modern technology" to "glorify lying, cheating, stealing, marital infidelity, and even murder."

Nonetheless, for the most part, the Washington archdiocese, and certainly our parish, seemed to cleave to an age-old Catholic tradition in America. Except on very few political issues with clear-cut moral and doctrinal relevance—today abortion, euthanasia, and the death penalty are foremost among them—the Catholic clergy, especially the rank-and-file, parish-based clergy, tends to maintain silence, leaving political decisions to the private consciences of parishioners.

Quietness of Heart

Did I regret our priests' reticence on this issue of national moment? In the end, no. At first I wondered about it. The Clinton matter, after all, raised not just political but significant moral concerns. But as I looked out on our suburban, middle-class congregation, brimming with young children, I could not imagine how our priests could raise the Lewinsky issue from the pulpit without making parents squirm in their pews. Moreover, comment on the scandal would have divided parishioners along political lines (this was, after all, predominantly Democratic Montgomery County, where political feelings on all sides tend to run strong).

Perhaps more to the point, for somebody who had spent entirely too many hours in 1998 watching talking heads on MSNBC and feeling outrage at the president and his defenders, the reprieve from "all Lewinsky, all the time" came as something of a relief.

Not only was the regular Sunday reprieve from the Clinton controversy welcome; it was also, I began to sense, necessary, as a prerequisite for spiritual health. Worship demands quietness of heart. "Be still, and know that I am God," says the Psalm. Much of the Catholic Mass is aimed at helping the soul to disengage from worldly cares, emotions, and sins in preparation for reception of the Eucharist, the body of Christ. Toward the end of this preparation, the congregation engages in the "sign of peace," in which the priest prays for the peace of Christ and worshippers offer a sign of peace, usually a handshake, to one another. It is this peace of Christ that we are exhorted to accept into our hearts during worship and then carry back out into our daily lives. As fallen human beings, all of us know how elusive this peace can be. One certainly does not find it in the political realm.

The Soul in Strife

Politics is not a spiritual activity. Indeed, it is among the least spiritual of activities, because it involves the soul in strife. Not that it is wrong; it is a vocation like any other. Nations need politics and politicians, and my own belief is that our nation is best served by having politicians who are themselves moral, upright, and genuinely religious, in whatever tradition. Moreover, strife, political and otherwise, is an unavoidable feature of earthly life. But the beginning of wisdom on the question of religion and politics—as St. Augustine knew—is the recognition that the two activities are antithetical in nature. Politics, based on self-love, engages and usually inflates the ego; religion, based on love of God, demands that we overcome it.

Jesus seemed unimpressed by the political sphere, almost contemptuous of it. When others attempted to draw him into the major political conflicts of his day, he resisted. Asked whether Jews should pay taxes to the Roman Empire—certainly a "hot-button" issue—he requested a coin and then inquired whose image was on it. Caesar's, came the reply. "Render therefore unto Caesar what is Caesar's," he said, "and to God what is God's." St. Paul's political advice to the early Church was essentially the same: it consisted largely in exhorting Christians to be law-abiding citizens and to respect temporal rulers as having been put in place by God. There was a great concern—first on the part of Jesus, later his apostle Paul—to prevent Christianity from becoming a merely political movement.

A too direct coupling of religion and politics in the public square is usually pernicious, not only for politics but also for religion itself. The result is typically not the sanctification of politics but the politicization of religion. When Christianity became the official religion of the Roman Empire, the Church left behind long years of persecution but also lost some of its original innocence in its new collaboration with the state. Indeed, the great scandals of Christian history have always been political scandals, stemming from the Church's use and abuse of temporal power.

Does God Take Sides?

Closer to home, no one could fail to notice how little help religion and religious language provided in sorting out the Clinton mess. At first, the matter of Clinton's lies and misdeeds seemed tailormade for the religious right, who jumped all over the issue. But soon Carole Shields of People for the American Way took to the airwaves announcing that she was the daughter of a Baptist preacher and urging the nation to ignore the president's misconduct and "move on." Once the right had draped its political views in the mantle of Christianity, the left was impelled to do the same.

The day before the impeachment vote in the House of Representatives, the president's own rather visible Methodist minister, J. Philip Wogaman, was on radio and television reminding us that Jesus preached "forgiveness." The political relevance of this lofty observation was hard to discern. Yes, Jesus loves the driver who speeds twenty miles over the limit, and ultimately, one hopes, forgives him, even if Jesus would prefer that the driver would behave himself. But does Jesus mean for us to let the speeder out of the traffic fines? Jesus, we are taught, can forgive murderers and child molesters and exhorts us too to forgive such people. But that does not relieve society of the necessity, or the duty, to define such acts as crimes and punish them accordingly.

The longer the debate went on, the more it seemed to me that the Clinton issue was best viewed through the purely secular lens of politics, law, and constitutionality. In this I am sure I am not alone. By the end of the president's virtuoso performance at September's National Prayer Breakfast—in which he concluded a lengthy and lugubrious confession of various "sins" with an angry pledge that his lawyers would fight the charges to the end—I am sure there were many Christian conservatives who were ready to rebuild the much-maligned "wall of separation" between church and state brick by brick.

Both sides in the House impeachment debate prominently invoked the name of God. Did God take sides in this great controversy? It would be presumptuous to assume so. God is not a sociologist, much less a pundit. We think in terms of collectivities and opinion polls. We, especially those of us involved in politics or public policy, attach great importance to the goings-on in the White House or on Capitol Hill. God—the Bible is very clear on this—does not see the world quite the way we do. Where we see collectivities and poll numbers, God sees individual hearts, their inmost thoughts and intentions. What we judge to be of great importance from our perspective in the earthly city—an impeachment debate, for example—may not have quite the same importance from the standpoint of the city of God.

We focus on collectivities, while God works one soul at a time. In this way He manages to bring about large results by means that are often invisible to us. A Roman pundit, circa 30 AD, would have certainly regarded the execution of a certain charismatic religious leader in Jerusalem as a politically marginal occurrence, a virtual nonevent. He would have had no idea that within 300 years, this event and its aftermath would transform the Roman Empire beyond recognition.

The Individual Conscience

Religion does its real work in politics not by arousing moral indignation but by awakening the individual conscience. The distinction is a subtle but important one. Moral indignation drives us to condemn others; conscience prompts us to question ourselves. The great leaps of progress in Western politics have come from an awakening of conscience. Indeed, viewed in the perspective of two millennia, the story of Western politics has been a tale of the progressive awakening of conscience, the application of an ever more exacting, humane, and—dare we say it? Christian moral standard to political life.

As Augustine observed, the "earthly city" and the "city of God," politics and religion, are separate and exist in opposition to each other. But the vision of the city of God has functioned as a kind of standing critique of the earthly city. And gradually, through the stepwise work of reason, the Western conscience has sought to bring life in the earthly city more in line with values of the heavenly city, and continues to do so.

In large measure, the society we have attempted to fashion in modern liberal democracies—a society, for example, that debates the impeachment of a leader based on offenses growing out of a sexual harassment lawsuit—is underpinned by values first set forth definitively in the New Testament. The notion of the God-given equal dignity and freedom of every individual human being—regardless of class, gender, race, or ethnic group—first appeared full-blown in the earliest Christian communities, some of which were not only unprecedentedly egalitarian but also unprecedentedly multiethnic in character. Amid the rigid social hierarchies and exclusionary religious and cultural taboos of the ancient world, Christianity offered a gentler, more radically egalitarian, and more multiethnic or colorblind view of the human being. "There is neither Jew nor Greek, there is neither slave nor free, there is neither male nor female," wrote Paul to the Galatians, "for you are all one in Christ Jesus." In the long run, Western history has been the tale of the gradual incorporation of this vision into politics—not by violent revolution but by a slow process of inward transformation.

The evolution of the Christian attitude to slavery illustrates the point. Augustine, like Paul, believed slavery to be a purely political matter and therefore of no concern for Christians. But Augustine was clearly embarrassed that some Christians held slaves and sought to defend their practice on grounds that Christian slaveholders treated slaves more humanely, more like family.

Later, when conditions changed, and slavery no longer played a functional or in any sense necessary role in increasingly industrial economies, the Christian world's "bad conscience" about slavery translated into action. The nineteenth-century antislavery movement (like, to a somewhat lesser extent, the twentieth-century civil rights movement) was religiously inspired but worked largely by appealing to the conscience of society, a conscience shaped by the vision of the city of God. Not that anger and indignation were absent from the debates over slavery and segregation: in America the division over slavery led to war. But leaders such as William Wilberforce, who spearheaded the peaceful British antislavery campaign, and Martin Luther King, Jr., who shepherded the nonviolent civil rights movement, self-consciously appealed to the consciences of their fellow citizens. Progress ultimately came less from external political conflict than from inward moral transformation, from human beings finally admitting to themselves that slavery and, later, racial discrimination were wrong. The gulf between social practice and Christian principle was finally understood to be intolerable.

America's Moral Advance

We have in recent years taken this vision of a free, equal, and tolerant society to new heights. Those who complain of pervasive moral decline in American society over the past generation often overlook an astonishing moral advance. We have gone farther than the human race has ever gone toward fashioning a society that guarantees, in practice as well as principle, the equal dignity of individuals regardless of race, class, creed, gender, or ethnic origin. There are still imperfections, still racisms, still tensions. But in all it is a remarkable transformation. I grew up in Chicago, once designated the most racially segregated city in the nation. Today I live in a multiracial, multiethnic middle-class neighborhood in Silver Spring, Maryland, where people of all colors and backgrounds are on mostly easy terms.

Human beings rarely get things quite right, and it is arguable that Americans have pushed the notion of tolerance too far. The public's response to the Clinton crisis is widely taken, by conservatives at least, as evidence of this fact. But the public's response to the Clinton matter is hopelessly entangled with other political feelings and ideas. And political assessments, as I have tried to suggest, often provide a terribly superficial guide to what is really taking place in society's soul. The signs are plenty that the tendency toward indiscriminate relativism and "nonjudgment-alism"—so ably documented by Alan Wolfe—is already self-correcting. For nearly a decade, Western thinkers, ranging from Michael Sandel and Amitai Etzioni to the pope, have been advancing a critique of "unbounded autonomy" or the "unencumbered self." More significantly, a rediscovery of religion and ethics is taking place at the individual level. To some degree, social statistics reflect this trend: Etzioni called attention some years ago to the "curl back" in the various leading social indicators, crime, teen pregnancy, and so forth, all of which continue their dramatic decline. But the most impressive reports come from the field, from religious leaders who

WWJD?

STACI SIMMONS

"WHAT WOULD JESUS DO?" may be the trendiest slogan among this generation of Christian youth in America. Its acronym, "WWJD?" adorns jewelry, clothing, coffee mugs, key chains, and school supplies, even a CD under the contemporary Christian music label of EMI. The original manufacturer of the inexpensive nylon bracelets that kicked off the pop-culture fashion has sold over 17 million of the bracelets alone.

This marketing boom began in 1997. Yet the WWJD? concept springs from an 1896 novel by Charles Sheldon entitled *In His Steps,* a book that has been translated into 45 languages and has never been out of print. It portrays an ordinary city at the turn of the century in an America replete with inner-city slums, rampant homelessness, and a complex system of social and economic hierarchy.

The respectable citizens in Sheldon's novel attend church each Sunday morning. They also ignore the social ills around them. The comfortable weekly routine of the faithful continues until, at the close of a sermon on following Jesus' example, a homeless, sick, and malnourished man makes his way to the front of the congregation. Standing before the mortified congregants, many of whom had previously turned down his pleas for a paying job, the man asks what it means to imitate Jesus. He wonders out loud about the connection between the words preached, the hymns sung, and his own experience with those who sit before him. He speaks of the world that might be born if Christians were to live out the words they speak each Sunday morning. But before he can finish, the man collapses and dies.

see changes in individual lives. Campus Crusade founder Bill Bright, for example, is convinced that a revival is under way, as is evangelist Steven Arterburn. Religion is reentering American life, not so much via the public square as through the back door, via the individual conscience. Individuals are rediscovering religion experientially, almost pragmatically, as the best solution to the real quandaries posed by modern life. I can see these forces at work at St. Peter's in Olney—which boasts a huge, enthusiastic congre-

So shaken are the fictional congregants and their minister that a large group pledges to live a full year asking themselves "what would Jesus do?" in the everyday situations of life. The group agrees to be guided solely by principles rooted in personal interpretations of the example of Jesus and His motivations, carefully studied. The experiment alters the lives of both the participants and their community.

The story picks up a century later. In the late 1980s, a youth minister in Holland, Michigan, commissioned two dozen inexpensive WWJD? wristbands to give to her youth group as a reminder of the challenge. The trinkets became increasingly popular around the city and caught on nationwide in 1997.

In effect, the marketers are enjoying great success through the mass distribution of a question. The popularity of WWJD? paraphernalia may rest precisely on the willingness—perhaps eagerness—of the sellers to leave the question's answer to individual purchasers. Yet Sheldon's message was indisputably both individual and social, entailing both moral transformation and compassion toward the needy.

America is in the midst of a spiritual renewal, as noted by Patrick Glynn and others in these pages. The success of the WWJD? phenomenon signals youth's role in that renewal. Now gauged primarily by its market impact, the extent of the trend's social influence will be measured in time by the answers, given both personally and communally, to the renewed interest in Sheldon's ageless question.

gation, a vibrant youth group, and a degree of spirituality, on the part of both priests and lay people, that was rare in the Catholicism of my youth. That's where the real action is, and that is what will shape the America of the future. I have little doubt my fellow parishioners were capable of drawing the right moral lesson from the Clinton scandal for themselves and their children, without a sermon or an official statement from the Church.

12

Judging the President

ALAN WOLFE

CONSIDERING THAT the problem of church and state goes back at least to the time that Jesus proposed a division of labor with Caesar, it can hardly be surprising that America has never quite settled the role that religion should play in public life. Indeed, if Americans can be said to have made distinctive contributions to the problem, they appear to run in exactly contradictory directions. On the one hand, our First Amendment, as interpreted by the Supreme Court, establishes a "wall" between church and state higher and more difficult to scale than those in other liberal democracies in western Europe, where established state churches can still be found. (Sweden abolished its official ties to Lutheranism only a couple of years ago.) On the other hand, Americans seem to be far more pious and churchgoing than Europeans; Swedes, once again for comparison's sake, tend to disdain the religiosity that pervades so many aspects of American public life.

Two hundred years after the brilliant writings of James Madison and Thomas Jefferson on the topic, Americans cannot make up their minds whether religion is primarily private, public, or some uneasy combination of the two. A generation ago the Warren Court issued pronouncements that seemed determined to root out even the faintest odors of religiosity from the public square. Recently, both President Clinton and those who sought his removal from office appealed to religious imagery to buttress their cases. If we are confused, however, we have good reason: religion is too much part of American self-identity ever to be ignored, especially by institutions that shape our identity as much as government institutions do. Yet nearly all efforts to bring religion and politics closer together seem to end badly, especially in a society populated by people who love God but hate politics.

The Theologians' Declaration

An indication of the difficulties one encounters in thinking through these questions is provided by the Declaration concerning Religion, Ethics, and the Crisis in the Clinton Presidency, in which more than 140 theologians protested what they called "the manipulation of religion and the debasing of moral language" surrounding the president's conduct before and after he met Monica Lewinsky. "We believe that serious misunderstandings of re-pentance and forgiveness are being exploited for political advantage," the declaration continued. "The resulting moral confusion is a threat to the integrity of American religion and to the foundations of a civil society."[1] The signatories were clearly bothered by President Clinton's repeated ex-pression of sorrow, which in their view asked for forgiveness without dem-onstrating any real repentance. They also felt that highly publicized meetings between the president and various spiritual advisers could result in reli-gious institutions providing "authentication" for the president's immoral behavior.

In bringing religious judgment to bear on a political issue, signatories to the declaration have no choice but to challenge that point of view which holds that faith is a private matter between an individual and his or her God while politics is a public matter involving all the bonds that hold us together as a people. Jean Bethke Elshtain, one of those who signed, ques-tions this point of view with her usual power and eloquence. How can we say that what the president did is in any way private, she asks in her chapter in *Judgment Day at the White House*, which published the theologians' dec-laration and various arguments defending and criticizing it. "Once a Presi-dent is elected, he is our President," she writes. "We may not have voted for him, but if he occupies the White House, then he is ours. We are called upon to respond to his appeals, especially when he commits American blood and treasure in times of war and crisis."[2]

To accept the idea that President Clinton can be an effective leader when he so clearly is a man of flawed character, Elshtain continues, indicates that "we have moved into a zone of amoral Machiavellianism that ill befits us as a people."[3] But is that necessarily bad? For a society to be one of which its members can be proud, it ought to have leaders who manifest such Christian virtues as humility and charity. Yet to survive, a society, even one governed by the rules of law, will from time to time require leaders whose character will make room for duplicity, dishonesty, even disrespect for human life. The great twentieth-century philosopher Isaiah Berlin once described Machiavelli's insight in this way: Florence could pursue the objective of being a Christian commonwealth or of being a great state but not both simultaneously. If goodness and ruthlessness are incompatible, however, modern societies have designed one method to allow them to coexist: the public/private distinction. As private individuals, we are free to strive to be as virtuous as our faith demands. As public officials, virtue must take its place along with other duties, some of them bordering on vice.

The failure to understand the difference between private and public conduct doomed the new left, whose slogan—the personal is the political—led directly to the tyranny of political correctness: if our innermost thoughts, what is most private about us, are subject to the scrutiny of the community to which we belong, then government is justified in regulating those thoughts in the public interest. Would the same illiberal consequences follow if we breach the public/private distinctions, not for reasons of politics, but instead for reasons of faith? I am afraid that the answer must be yes.

Which Religious Values?

Any attempt to judge political leaders by the standards of religious values raises the question of which values will be used. The declaration, in a bow to America's religious pluralism, endorses "the public mission of our churches, synagogues, and mosques." Yet not a single one of the signatories is affiliated with a Jewish or Moslem institution, and all the contributors to

Judgment Day make arguments rooted in Christian theology. And even that narrowing of the scope of religion does not help them answer the question of whose morality ought to stand in judgment over the president. For the contributors to *Judgment Day* are both Catholic and Protestant. Not only are there differences between them, but each tradition has its own differences within: Southern Baptists have a different take on morality than Episcopalians, and, as William J. Buckley's chapter in *Judgment Day* makes clear, Catholics are as split on the issue within the faith as are any other group of Americans. One reason to preserve the public-private distinction, in short, is because it holds in check whatever inclination we may have to insist that our values ought to be everyone's values.

In response to this problem, the president can be held accountable to the religious values of his own faith, a task best undertaken by those who share that faith. Yet while this solution avoids the problem of religious diversity, signers of the declaration find it unsatisfactory. At the Religious Leaders Prayer Breakfast last September 11, President Clinton acknowledged that he had sinned and announced that he would "continue on the path of repentance seeking pastoral support and that of other caring people so that they can hold me accountable for my own commitment." As is well known, the president met with a number of ministers, including J. Philip Wogaman, pastor of the Foundry United Methodist Church, the very church the Clintons usually attend. (Wogaman himself has written on Christian ethics.) By insisting that none of this is sufficient, signers of the declaration put themselves in an extremely awkward position, for not only are they judging Clinton's actions, they are also judging the depths of his religious beliefs. On this point, many of the contributors to Judgment Day could not go along. Nicholas Wolterstorff, a philosopher and theologian at Yale University, wrote that we should "rejoice over the sinner who returns home," not "react with sour grumpiness" to his presumed insincerity.[4]

Signers of the declaration, however much they agree on the need to hold the president accountable, do not agree on their political views; some make it clear that they voted for Clinton, others indicate their support for positions rooted in their faith (opposition to abortion or the death penalty, greater economic and social justice) that the president does not share or shares only partially, and others sound not dissimilar from the House Re-

publican managers in the impeachment trial. This diversity of viewpoint
suggests that the declaration has little in common with—and in fact seems
at many points quite hostile to—groups and individuals identified with
the Christian right. The Christian Coalition, for example, believes that
religion cannot be divorced from morality and that morality cannot be
kept apart from politics, whereas the declaration only states that "politics
and morality cannot be separated," a far less contentious proposition. Because they avoid the extremism of the religious right, signers of this declaration are not put in the position of saying that the American people, who
have insisted all along that Clinton should not be removed from office, are
somehow immoral. (One exception is Stanley Hauerwas, who writes that
"Bill Clinton is what we should expect, given our politics.")[5] Down that
road lies an eventual attack on democracy, as if any conflict between popular opinion and the truth known by people of faith has to be resolved in
favor of the latter.

If Not the People, Who?

Yet if the president must be judged, someone must do the judging. Instead
of the people, the signers of the declaration offer themselves. There are,
writes Max Stackhouse of the Princeton Theological Seminary, spin doc-
tors whose job it is to defend the president. But then there are public intellectuals and public theologians who violate their professional duties if they
"adjust judgments to short-term political effects."[6] The real task of such
individuals, he continues, is to "identify, clarify, and enhance the deeper
structures of justice in and for our common life when things are messy." In
a similar way, Jean Elshtain argues that the president's behavior "must be
scrutinized critically by those charged with particular responsibility for evaluating the role of religion in public life, and public life in light of religion."[7]

   I think both writers are correct to emphasize the importance of public
intellectuals in offering dispassionate criticism of public life, for there are
indeed few other places from which such criticism can come. But I also
think that when one offers himself for that role, one ought to do so with
humility. (I leave for others to judge whether I have always followed my

own advice here; somehow I doubt that I have.) The task of the social critic is, to be sure, to criticize, but the best criticism, as Michael Walzer has emphasized, is usually that which takes pains to identify with and understand what is under scrutiny.[8] I am not suggesting that Stackhouse and Elshtain should have put themselves in President Clinton's shoes, nor even in those of the American public. But I do think it correct to emphasize that when two-thirds of the American people hold a viewpoint different from that of the critic, the latter is under more of an obligation to examine his or her own assumptions than the signers of this declaration seem to demonstrate. I say this as someone who, for much of his political life, did take positions with which most Americans disagreed. Trying to understand why they did so was the first step which brought me from somewhere out in left field politically to my wishy-washy place in the center today.

If there is fault to be found with the signers of the declaration for finding too easy an application of religious values to public issues, ought one not also fault the president for invoking religious language in his own defense? Surely one must, although it cannot be on the terms established by the declaration. Clinton is in the business of being judged; as a politician, he has subjected himself to the judgment of the electorate many times. To be sure, he is not eligible to run for president once his term is over, and he is unlikely to run for anything else. But that does not give him liberty to seek the judgment of God or his fellow parishioners in highly visible, seemingly orchestrated, ways. I can fully understand why the signatories to the declaration took offense at the president's public displays of his piety. I did as well. But if we find the way he practices politics problematic, we can only seek a political recourse. In its own way, that is what the signatories did, for in collecting signatures, publishing a book, and seeking press coverage of their efforts, they were, however sincere their faith, also engaged in a political effort. It only cheapens the importance of what they believe for them to invoke religious language on their behalf, for in so doing, they have met the president they so strongly disdain more than halfway.

13

A Response to Alan Wolfe

MAX L. STACKHOUSE

ALAN WOLFE'S REVIEW of *Judgment Day at the White House*, to which I was a contributor, requires response on three points.

First, Wolfe seems to have projected a "boomer" attempt to collapse the personal into the political onto the intent of the volume. But in fact what prompted our rather open and multivoiced debate was precisely the way in which the personal and the political were combined by the president through the invocation of religious themes in relation to legal ones. Our first concern is not political or personal but ethical and social. Indeed, Wolfe has argued elsewhere that basic moral and spiritual perceptions and not only practical considerations shape political institutions as well as personal character. Since religion is often the bearer of these perceptions, our debate was about the ethical and spiritual appeals that can legitimately be made if religion is publicly used.

Second, Wolfe makes too little distinction between religion and theology and seems to understand theology as nothing more than the articulated expression of a particular religion's biases. It is true that some religious leaders understand theology this way and can properly be said to view it as a kind of megaphone for particular confessional interests. However, growing clusters of "public theologians" understand theology to be a critical, comparative, evaluative discipline, one able to assess the relative merits of differing religious confessions, doctrines, and practices—much in the way

96

in which good political scientists can assess the relative merits of platforms and policies of various parties or good economists might analyze the viability of a number of national economies. None of these is likely to be totally neutral or entirely devoid of loyalty to particular perspectives, but all of these—political scientists, economists, and public theologians alike—seek to speak from standpoints that are publicly accessible and not privileged by nondebatable presumptions.

Third, if religious matters have long-range sociocultural consequences, and if theology can best be understood as a necessary discipline in assessing them, it surely is important that theologians must seek to inform the public and form public opinion regarding the gravity of the issues that may not fully be seen by the public. Indeed, it seems more "democratic" to debate the issues openly than to have religious authorities issue uncontestable ethical conclusions or sociologists articulate the views already most widely held in political process. That is what we did—in a form that has more self-criticism and modesty than the critics of theology usually acknowledge or display.

14

The Clinton Scandal and the Culture of the Therapeutic

JEAN BETHKE ELSHTAIN

I HAVE LONG stressed in my work that it is vital to the workings of a democratic society to avoid conflating public and private. From *Public Man, Private Woman: Women in Social and Political Thought* in 1981 to *Democracy on Trial* in 1995, I have insisted that it is disastrous to presume that the personal simply is the political. My target was the presumption in much radical and liberal-left feminism of the 1970s (and that heritage perdures) that pushed a thorough-going politicization of personal and private life. In so doing, such thinkers and activists, or so I argued, wound up privatizing public life. For if there are no distinctions between public and private, personal and political, it follows that no differentiated activity that is genuinely political, that pertains to the "commons" and has to do with the ordering and purpose of a political community, exists. Instead, personal and political are collapsed as an identity of each to the other is promoted. Nothing personal in this scheme of things is exempt from political definition, direction, and manipulation. This is not only incoherent—as human beings have always been creatures who make vital distinctions and develop categories to distinguish some aspects of life from others—it makes for very bad politics indeed. One hallmark of twentieth-century totalitarian orders was precisely their regimented collapse of personal into an overarching political order that destroyed politics. Why? Because, again, if everything is political, nothing is—there is no way to mark an area called "politics" that is the purview of citizens, of human beings in their identities as civic beings.

That said, it is also the case that it makes no sense in a democracy to presuppose an absolute chasm or bright line separating public and private. The task, rather, is to assess just how and in what ways public and private, personal and political, are or ought to be related. To refuse to collapse personal and political doesn't commit one to a rigid bifurcation between the two, a binary opposition. What one needs is a set of criteria that helps in sorting out how the political flows into our personal lives and how private activities, in turn, flow outward, affecting politics directly and indirectly. Much of democratic theory historically has been devoted to sorting this question out. A nuanced feminism attempts the same sort of delicate teasing out of relationships. American law is charged with the task of assessing what is public and what is private all the time. These are not hermetically sealed-off categories. For in each realm people sort out meaning and enact projects that diminish or enhance their capacities to love, to work, to participate, to be decent and caring friends, neighbors, and parents as they participate in a variety of ways in the layered communities of which they are a part. In late modernity, there is no aspect of our lives that is simply left untouched by politics. I tell my students, "You may not be interested in politics. But politics is definitely interested in you." Similarly, it is difficult to think of a private or personal activity that might not have *some* implications for a wider community, by which I mean a community beyond that of one's immediate circle of intimates. So: how do we sort this out? Particularly in cases of conflict. Particularly in instances of disagreement about whether what is going on is "my" business, or "our" business.

Given my criticisms of President Clinton's behavior and the role I played as one of the signatories and most public defenders of the *Declaration concerning Religion, Ethics, and the Crisis in the Clinton White House*, have I radically shifted my position as defender of the distinction between the public and the private? Not at all. Why? To put it very simply, because the president's behavior was public all along. What happens in the Oval Office is by definition a public matter. This is the workplace of our most public person: the president of the United States. It is not a love nest in the Poconos. It is not a pick-up bar. It is an office for our most public of office holders. Although the signatories of the declaration didn't take this up explicitly, it figured importantly in my own thinking. Overwhelmingly, all of the sign-ers (and they numbered 230 or so by the time we shut down our web site) were concerned, saddened, even angered by what we considered an inap-propriate use (and abuse) of religion as a tool deployed to evade, rather than to confront, one's responsibilities as a believer, a citizen, and, most important, the holder of an *office*. We rightly expect and demand more from holders of certain offices by contrast to others. Some people have much more strenuous and demanding public responsibilities. What goes on between a bar owner and a cocktail waitress by way of "consensual" sexuality may trouble us, but it doesn't *concern* us as citizens. The bar owner's office hasn't the same educative and public responsibility as does that of the president of a university or the president of the United States. Our expec-tation concerning the range of reasonable and suitable behavior varies from office to office. This doesn't mean there is a "different" moral standard for some persons compared with others; it does mean there is a different set of ethical expectations and political implications for persons as disparate of-fice holders. Adultery is adultery. But sexual recklessness or fecklessness may or may not be a matter for appropriate political concern, critique, and assessment. That depends. Who did what, when, where, and how.

The *how* is critical. If one's sexual misdeeds are grubby (and one is president of the United States and the deeds took place in one's place of work and involved a low-level employee), that's bad enough. But if the misdeeds required implicating everyone from secretary to spouse to secre-tary of state to the Secret Service in cover-up, possible legal culpability, and lying, then by any ethical standard of which I know anything this is not only serious, it is politically fraught. Responsible leaders do not mislead, lie to, and knowingly implicate their staffs in acts that put those with whom they work and on whom they rely at serious risk; that involves abusing and misusing those whose loyalty is relied on. As David Broder put it, "The president trashed the place and it wasn't his to trash." My students at the University of Chicago were most concerned with the knowing misuse of so many people in such demeaning activities, and so was I.

The problem of the abuse of religion in public life in this matter does not involve questions of separation of church and state or severing religion from politics altogether. As all students of American religion know, separation of church and state is one thing. Separation of religion and politics is something else altogether. Religion and politics flow back and forth in American civil society all the time—always have, always will. How could it be otherwise? Too much of the same public territory is claimed by each: membership in a community; formation of responsible selves who have a communal and not just self-serving ethos; public modes of expression and action (going to church isn't a secret activity, after all); creating and sustaining institutions that serve communities—schools, hospitals, soup kitchens, day care centers, elder care centers, on and on. So faith is always a public declaration. That's what Bar Mitzvah or confirmation is about: a coming of age; a ritual; a public presentation of a "self" to a community; and public recognition of that self as a member of a community that gives public voice to its identity in a society like our own with freedom of religious exercise.

Although one strand of fideistic Protestantism views faith as a private matter of conscience between an individual and his or her God, churches bring such persons together. As well, there is strong communally oriented congregationalism, the robust ecclesiology of Catholicism, and the public rituals of a temple are not private matters at all. What is "private"—although that term doesn't really grasp what is at stake—is "freedom of conscience." What I mean by "private" here is that this cannot and must not be coerced by public or political authorities. But no individual would even have an idea of what "faith" meant in the absence of *communities* of the faithful. Those who describe faith in a radically privatized way are more likely to accept behavior such as that exhibited by President Clinton, who simultaneously declared both his "private life"—as a term to cover grubby doings, in this instance—and his religion off-limits to public scrutiny. Yet, at the same time, such commentators are likely to fall silent before this president's or any president's public use of both family and religion if it serves his purposes—so long as those are political positions shared by the commentators. Those of us who see faith as a public activity, made manifest in the presence of others, are more likely to question the uses made of religion for public purposes, whether by an individual or group, no matter whose ox is being gored. That is, for us these determinations are matters of principle, not ideology.

In one of my essays on the Clinton mess I argued that if one creates a wall of separation between ethics and politics, one effects an "amoral Machiavellianism" of the sort that corrupts democratic politics over time. Democracy relies heavily on trustworthiness and legitimacy. If people doubt every word a leader says and have concluded that "his word cannot be trusted" (because he is a person of "low moral character" who has demonstrated his untrustworthiness), then he "cannot do his job effectively." I believe strongly that this is the case: that a leader under such circumstances cannot put together the domestic coalitions he requires to conduct the people's business in anything other than a fly-by-the-seat-of-your-pants, ad hoc way, and that is indeed what we have seen. To be sure, one can reach the sad conclusion that a particular leader is untrustworthy, knowing that it does not follow automatically that there is an easy answer about what should be done. That is, one might arrive at the conclusion I did about President Clinton's behavior but not conclude that removal from office is the appropriate remedy.

The important conceptual point, however, is that one cannot drive a wedge between ethics and politics. None of our great democratic leaders has ever done that. The declaration accepts explicitly that "extreme dangers sometimes require a political leader to engage in morally problematic actions. But we maintain that in general there is a reasonable threshold of behavior beneath which our public leaders should not fall." We added, "Neither we nor our students demand perfection." The point is that the "amoral Machiavellianism" *cannot become a rule of thumb, just the way things get done around here.* That would have a debilitating effect on democratic public life. Such "Machiavellianism" should be occasional and occasioned by an unusual or serious threat of some sort and never be held up as normative by contrast to necessary. I, for one, am far less worried about character flaws than reckless deeds that may have public consequences. I believe the president's deeds did have such consequences: the Christmas bombings of Iraq would be one case in point. The public, overwhelmingly, refused to accept the president's demurrers that the timing of this campaign was in no way influenced by the impeachment imbroglio. Please recall that the attack began the day before the impeachment debate in the House was scheduled to begin and ended a few hours after the House voted to impeach. The public's skepticism and the timing of this matter show clearly a spill-over between irresponsible deeds proclaimed as "private" and public attitudes and consequences. So: the question, once again, is sorting out when "private" flows into and (in this case) taints or tilts "public" and vice versa. To argue that this is what needs to be thought about seriously is not to confuse private and public conduct. It is, instead, to ask what the relationship between conduct in different spheres and to different ends and purpose may be. None of us lives in walled-off boxes so that there is no spill-over of any kind between one arena and the other. As Sissela Bok has argued in her major book on truth telling, lying is rarely something that generates a discrete, containable effect. Patterns of deceit corrode ever-widening circles, depending, again, on the nature of the deceit and the nature of the venue and the actors.

No one who signed the declaration was interested in ferreting out anybody else's bad thoughts. Deeds alone were at issue. Public declarations of one's "private" faith are not private matters; they are public matters. You have made them public when you go public. There are consequences to be reckoned with, therefore. Some critics of *Judgment Day at the White House* questioned why there were no Jewish and Muslim signatories. Our response was that their religion was not implicated in this matter in the same public way as was Christianity. We believed it was our responsibility to respond, as it was the Christian faith that the president called upon. It was the Christian faith that was dragged into the matter by the president and his staffers and spinners and publicists who planned a whole operation around the prayer breakfast confession–after doing polling to see if a confession of "sin" would fly. It would be a dereliction of public responsibility not to respond if one believed there was something seriously inappropriate about the use of the prayer breakfast for self-exculpation, particularly when the president never accepted responsibility for his deeds publicly. He said he was sorry. But he always reverted to the passive voice—"people have been hurt"—rather than claiming agency in the matter. And in the matter of most concern within Christian ethics—the ill use of so many people; not

chastity, therefore, but a form of fecklessness or cowardice—the president
never stepped up to the plate at all. When the president spoke of diplo-
matic efforts surrounding Middle East peace as evidence for his "journey
of repentance," it set the theologians' teeth on edge for sure. Why? Because
engaging in diplomacy is part of a president's job description: that is what
we elect him to do. In layering a confessional moment over that activity, it
was the president who was overpersonalizing the political, not the signers
of the declaration.

No one who signed the declaration presumed to judge the president's
beliefs. It was, to repeat, deeds that were in question—or misdeeds, in this
case. Clinton opened himself up to evaluation along religious lines because
he called upon religious categories to evade the public and political dimen-
sions of what he had done. He publicized religion and in so doing privatized politics. In a sense, he was saying, There are no standards of public
assessment that can be brought to bear appropriately in evaluating what I
did and how I did it because I am a "sinner." I, therefore, state that I am a
sinner (to a Christian theologian or ethicist this is no big revelation as all
have sinned and fallen short) and, in effect, that is the end of the matter.
This was a way to short-circuit an appropriate public debate. What sorts of
standards do we expect from public officials? Where do these standards
come from? In our view, the standards are those ethical values that lie at the
heart of conduct for the holder of a public office: prudence, loyalty, trustworthiness. And the public was with us in this—overwhelmingly so. (In
fact, about half of the public now believes that impeaching the president
was the right thing to do–something we took no stand on.) The vast majority judged the president's behavior quite severely, even though they didn't
want him removed from office. The signatories of the declaration thought
to deepen this ethical uneasiness in the interest of promoting deliberation
on serious questions: what is the relationship between public and private in
the Clinton case? What ought the relationship to be in an ideal sense?
What are reasonable expectations for ethical behavior on the part of public
officials? What unreasonable?

It is one thing for a president—as Abraham Lincoln did—to call up
the prophetic insistence that all the nations are under divine judgment and
quite another for a president—as Clinton did—to confess to sin with the

cameras whirring and a captive group of silent clergy as witnesses. This latter maneuver has a lot more to do with the triumph of a "therapeutic culture" that functions in an exculpatory way than with the appropriate bringing of religion to the public square. To raise questions concerning the inappropriate politicization of faith is what democratic citizens who take their responsibilities seriously are obliged to do. One of our major concerns was that the political intelligence should not be turned off once "personal sin" is publicly announced, especially not in a religiously plural culture in which citizen are not members of a single confessional community. These, then, were the exigent matters that compelled the signers of the declaration to step forward. Interestingly enough, a majority of the American public seems, following nearly a year of debate and deliberation, to concur, if the most recent surveys are reliable. We who signed the declaration do not take this as knock-down validation of our views but rather as a hopeful indication that, once the thunder and lightning have passed, American citizens are quite capable of evaluating the complexity and nuance of an issue such as this. Let's hope so, for these sorts of questions are not going away any time soon.

15

Errant Evangelical?
A Presidential Counselor in the Line of Fire

TONY CAMPOLO

IN CHRISTENDOM some of the most angry criticism of President Clinton comes from the evangelical community. Because I am part of that community, I have encountered some intense negative responses to my becoming one of his spiritual advisers. Almost immediately after the news broke about my involvement with the president, David Black, the president of Eastern College, where I teach, began getting phone calls from irate alumni and financial supporters of the college. Even some of my faculty colleagues joined the angry chorus, claiming that my association with President Clinton would corrupt the good name of the college. In the face of these reactions, I offered Black my resignation, which he rejected.

In the days and weeks that followed, Black stood behind my decision to counsel President Clinton. It remains to be seen whether the college will suffer further damage. My fear is that my continued presence on the faculty will lead some pastors to discourage their young congregants from considering Eastern as a place to study.

Several regular contributors to EAPE/Kingdomworks, an evangelical missionary organization with which I am also associated (in an unpaid position), wrote to let me know that they would be discontinuing their giving to our ministries to "at risk" children and teenagers in urban America, Haiti, and the Dominican Republic. I worry that a host of other contributors may stop giving without taking the time to write to me about their decision. Yet another concern is that my involvement with the president will cut off my opportunities to speak at evangelical college chapel services, a primary source of new recruits for our EAPE/Kingdomworks ministries. These days, it is a rare night that I do not wake and pace the floor, praying that our ministries will not suffer because of what I have decided to do.

Dealing with the Press

Each year in Washington representatives of America's various religious traditions meet with the president for a prayer breakfast to discuss ways in which the government and religious institutions can work together for the public good. Joan Brown Campbell, the executive director of the National Council of Churches, and several others suggested that the gathering last year, on September 11, would be a good forum for the president to confess his sins in the Monica Lewinsky affair and to ask for forgiveness. President Clinton did just that, calling what he had done "sin." As a basis for his remarks, the president used Psalm 51, written by King David after his adultery, pleading that God "cleanse" him and help purify his heart. President Clinton told the American people that he also would be asking God to "cleanse" him and make him into a "new" person. What he had to say, in words reflecting the religiosity of his Southern Baptist background, moved him well beyond referring to what he had done as "inappropriate behavior." The president also said that he had chosen a small group of clergymen to meet with him regularly and help him on his path of repentance. He deliberately did not announce who they were.

The prayer breakfast proved a major media event. Following the Friday morning breakfast there was widespread speculation as to whom the president had chosen for this pastoral responsibility. From the beginning, Gordon MacDonald, pastor of Grace Chapel in Lexington, Massachusetts, and one of the other clergymen chosen to be part of the president's accountability group, and I decided to say nothing to the press and keep as low a public profile as possible. The third member of the group, J. Philip Wogaman, pastor of the Foundry United Methodist Church in Washington, D.C., where the president usually attends Sunday worship, made a similar decision.

On Saturday evening Gordon MacDonald phoned and told me that the *Boston Globe* was planning to send a reporter to his Sunday morning worship service and that the local television stations would also be sending camera crews. We both realized that there would be no escape from public notoriety. We decided to issue brief press releases acknowledging that we were the clergy whom the president had chosen and stating that, given our pastoral obligations, we would be giving no interviews.

As I soon discovered, if you do not tell the press who you are, they come up with definitions of their own. On the following Tuesday morning, the *New York Times* ran a front-page story headlined "Clinton Selects Clerics to Give Him Guidance," in which journalist Laurie Goodstein defined me as "a liberal Baptist, who advocates that Christians accept homosexuality." Her story was quickly picked up by the Associated Press and sent around the world. By the next day, most newspapers were repeating her description of me verbatim.

The label "liberal" is anathema in evangelical Christian circles, as I was soon to be reminded. By Wednesday afternoon, my office was flooded with e-mail, faxes, and phone calls from "concerned Evangelicals" alarmed over my new designation. Because many who contacted my office were part of the vital financial base of our various ministries, my first concern was to keep the EAPE/Kingdomworks ministries out of serious trouble.

I called Goodstein at the *New York Times* to learn the source of her description of me. She recalled that she had met me once and remembered my opposition to efforts by the religious right to deny homosexuals some basic civil rights. She recalled my opposition to the welfare reform bill. She knew that I was part of the Call to Renewal, a broad-based Christian alternative to the politics of the Christian Coalition.

I explained that my refusal to embrace the political stance of the Christian Coalition on every issue did not mean that I was a liberal Baptist. I pointed out that many theologically conservative Baptists define themselves—as I do—as politically moderate. And I made clear that despite my concern for the civil rights of homosexuals, homosexual marriage is contrary to my understanding of Scripture.

Two days later the *Times* printed a correction. But a brief comment on page two could not undo what had been spread around the world on page one. Even people whom I know and consider brothers in Christ began repeating the *Times* report.

One such was Cal Thomas, a columnist for the *Los Angeles Times* and a spokesperson for the religious right, who is viewed by Evangelicals as the voice of truth in the distorting secular media. When he too called me "a liberal Baptist" who recently "has been urging conservative Christians to accept homosexuality," I phoned to contest the labels. He refused to explain why he had called me a liberal Baptist and said that he believed me to be "too close to the line" that separates those who oppose gay and lesbian marriages and those who affirm them. Some evangelical pastors used Thomas's article as all the evidence they needed to lambaste me from their pulpits. Christian talk shows on religious radio stations also used his column to condemn me.

Another was Pat Robertson, who had interviewed me on the *700 Club* a few years earlier and at whose university I had been a chapel speaker. On the evening of September 15, a news report on his *700 Club* repeated the comments made about me in the *New York Times*, further damaging my standing among Evangelicals.

Wherever I went as a speaker on the evangelical circuit during the weeks that followed, even in Northern Ireland and Brazil, I had to explain myself to pastors and congregations. Indeed, I have come to expect that I will have to justify to evangelical audiences my claim that I am still one of them. Three large evangelical gatherings have canceled my speaking engagements. I was allowed to speak at the 1998 convention of the Southern Baptists of Tennessee and at an American Baptist gathering in West Virginia, though angry pastors protested my place on both programs.

Although more moderate groups, such as mainline denominations, are now inviting me to address their gatherings, it remains to be seen how my involuntary "repositioning" as a speaker will affect the ministries that my evangelical speaking tours helped support.

A Mistake

When I learned that *Time* and *Newsweek* magazines would be featuring major stories on the president's clerical advisers, I contacted reporters there to try to curtail further damage from misinformation. Kenneth Woodward's *Newsweek* article dealt with our theology, trying to understand how our beliefs about grace and forgiveness might influence the way in which we related to the president. The *Time* article was less kind, describing me—ironically, it seemed to me—as being "media savvy" and suggesting that I was trying to further my career as a "motivational speaker."

Still trying to find a way to reassure the people across the country who know me that I was not what *Time* and the *New York Times* had made me out to be, I agreed to do an interview with Peggy Wehmeyer to be shown on Peter Jennings's news show and on 20/20. I had known Wehmeyer, an evangelical Christian who had done several television stories on our missionary work, for more than five years. When Gordon MacDonald indicated that he too was favorably disposed to an interview with her, I readily consented. We had turned down invitations from dozens of talk shows and news shows, but I thought that doing just this one spot would enable me to correct misconceptions and then end my dealings with the media.

In the interview we did our best not to say anything to suggest what happens during our sessions with the president, but I now think that the interview chipped away at our efforts to maintain perfect pastoral confidentiality. Certainly, the airing of the interview brought some accusatory letters. In the weeks that followed, everywhere I went to preach or lecture, reporters in the audience would seize on what I said from the pulpit to try to apply it to my conversations with the president. I have finally learned, I think, how to tailor my speaking accordingly.

Using Religion

Meanwhile, the Internet too had become my enemy. At least 3,000 articles, most derogatory and many declaring me to be an enemy of true Christianity, were readily available to anyone with a computer. Friends also informed me that the Internet had been used by a large group of academic theologians to issue a declaration condemning the president for the way he had repented of his sins and contending that his calling on pastors as an accountability group was cheapening the nature of true repentance. Suggest-

ing that the president was merely trying to provide some religious buttress-
ing to a weakened presidency, they proposed that the only evidence of true
repentance would be his resignation from office.

Though all the signers of the declaration appeared not to trust the
president's three clerical advisers to follow through with their understanding of the biblical requisites in the face of sin, not one had followed the
injunction in Matthew 18 that if Christians are concerned that brothers or
sisters are in error, they should go to them directly and confront them
personally. Still, I am open to the possibility that the signers' declaration
may well contain some important warnings. Religion can be used for political purposes. There is a tendency in our society to cheapen the repentance process to nothing more than a contrite declaration of "I'm sorry."

Prayers for the President

Time has passed since the president asked me to serve him as a spiritual
adviser. Still the letters come, many condemning, others affirming, encouraging, and grateful that I have made myself available to the president during a time of national crisis. Often support comes from unexpected sources.
For instance, Jerry Falwell, in a phone conversation, let me know that he
was praying for us daily in the hope that God's will for the president would
be done through us. As I go across the country, people regularly let me
know their opinions on what I am doing, and, again, many assure me that
they are praying for my ministry to the president.

One thing is certain. My involvement in what one newscaster called
"the most difficult pastoral responsibility in the world" has changed my
life forever. Once referred to by some, flatteringly, as "prophetic," now I
am known as a spiritual adviser to the president. To many my new mission appears to compromise my strong evangelical stance. The criticism
pushes me harder to do what has been given me to do with all zeal and
faithfulness.

PART FOUR
Faith-Based Social Action

16

The Third Stage
New Frontiers of Religious Liberty

E. J. DIONNE JR.

Two of our leading presidential candidates, Texas governor George W. Bush and Vice President Al Gore, are talking enthusiastically about what government can do to help "faith-based organizations" solve social problems. At a White House prayer breakfast with religious leaders in September 1999, President Clinton embraced what he called "an emerging consensus about the ways in which faith organizations and our government can work together." Pastors dealing with social problems are landing on the covers of national magazines, and scholars are predicting a new "great awakening" of religious fervor in the country.

What's going on here? Is the wall between church and state tumbling down?

Not at all. But the turn of the millennium in America may well be remembered as a time when the country renegotiated the relationship between religion and public life, faith and culture. Don't be scared by this: We are not about to chuck religious freedom, impose censorship, or herd everyone into a church, synagogue, or mosque. Indeed, it is partly because of advances in religious freedom—the result of court decisions and cultural changes during the 1960s—that it is even possible to talk about increased cooperation between the religious and governmental worlds.

There is no consensus yet on how church and state are supposed to work together, let alone how much. This is nothing new. Arguments for strong barriers between religion and government have waxed and waned through American history, for radically different reasons in different times.

Separation between church and state never meant that religion had no place in American life; remember, this is a nation that still stamps "In God We Trust" on its currency. But the rise of the religious conservatives and the culture wars of the past two decades sharpened the debate over separation and aroused both sides.

On the one side, religious conservatives decried the growing "secularization" of America and engaged in what sociologist Nathan Glazer has called a "defensive offensive" meant to restore the consensus on values that existed—or at least seemed to exist—before the sixties.[1] On the other, those dismayed by the religious right saw separation as a bulwark against the growing influence of organizations such as the Christian Coalition and the Moral Majority.

Many rank-and-file evangelical Christians found themselves as turned off as the rest of the country by polarization around political issues related to religion. "There's a certain backlash against the shrill, partisan message they've heard," Nathan Hatch, the provost at Notre Dame University and a historian of evangelical Christianity, told a conference organized by the Ethics and Public Policy Center in September 1999. "A lot of Evangelicals are suburban people, and they much more easily identify with a George Bush than a Jerry Falwell or a Gary Bauer. They're people of values. They're also tolerant. There's a sense that the attack mode is counterproductive."

The church-state divide has often been cast as a fight between religious people and their secularist foes. But out of the public eye, a lively argument is taking place among religious leaders about the wisdom of allowing any breach of the church-state wall.

There was once a time when the separation of church and state was a cardinal commandment of Southern Baptists and nearly all evangelical Protestants. For most of these Protestants, spending even a dime of public money on religious schools or church programs was to assail the founders, destroy religious freedom, and turn God into a servant of the state.

"Most people think church-state separationists are atheists or humanists or just bad people," said Derek Davis, director of the J. M. Dawson

Institute of Church-State Studies at Baylor University. "It's just not that way at all."

Davis's center at Baylor, one of the country's premier Baptist institutions, speaks for the old separationist tradition that still finds many adherents in the pews of Baptist churches. He offers useful reminders that the current argument over the role of religion in public institutions—especially in the public schools—has its roots early in American history. In 1844, he notes, six people were killed in a riot in Philadelphia over what version of the Ten Commandments should be posted in the public schools. Whatever one thinks of today's battles over whether to post the Ten Commandments in government buildings, nothing that disturbing has happened yet.

If all evangelical Christians thought like the old-line Baptist separationists, Clinton and other politicians probably wouldn't be talking so rapturously about a new relationship between church and state. But the culture wars changed the church-state argument by moving many Baptists and Evangelicals to a new view: that separation was promoting secularism and turning once-friendly public institutions into environments hostile to religion. The Reverend Richard John Neuhaus captured this sense in his 1984 book, *The Naked Public Square.*[2]

Thus, on church-state issues, says Richard Cizik, director of the Washington office of the National Association of Evangelicals (NAE), his organization has "really done a 180 [-degree turn]" over the past forty years. Once opposed to state aid to religious schools, Cizik said, the NAE now supports private school vouchers and has endorsed the "charitable choice" provisions of the 1996 welfare bill promoting government aid to faith-based charities.

Earlier in our history, arguments over separation were just as fierce but had different inspirations. When Catholic immigrants began flooding America from Ireland in the 1840s, there was strong Protestant opposition to any government assistance to the schools the Catholics were establishing. Here separationism was less about protecting government or religion than opposing any expansion of "popery."

Similar fights broke out from the late forties through the sixties over government aid to parochial schools. Eleanor Roosevelt carried out a fa-

mous and bitter public argument with New York's Cardinal Spellman on
the issue.

"Certainly there's been a regrettable history of animus toward Catholics," says Melissa Rogers, associate general counsel at the Baptist Joint
Committee on Public Affairs, whose group is separationist and spun off
from Southern Baptist Convention after Baptist conservatives defeated
moderates and liberals.

Davis agrees that separatism was often "fueled by this anti-Catholic
bias." But both Davis and Rogers insist that anti-Catholicism was less important historically to separationists than a general fear of the effect of state
involvement in religion on both government and the faith institutions
themselves.

What's striking now is that conservative Protestants who long opposed
aid to Catholic schools find themselves allied with Catholics on the voucher
issue. "One of the most remarkable changes of the twentieth century is the
virtual evaporation of hostility between Protestants and Catholics," says
Grant Wacker, a professor of religious history at Duke University Divinity
School. "I don't think it's because Baptists have come to have a great respect
for Tridentine theology. It's because they see Catholics as allies against graver
problems. There's a large reconfiguration going on now."

Indeed. In the separationist wars, separationist Baptists find themselves
allied with Jews and many mainline Protestant churches. But even more
relevant are liberal-conservative splits within the denominations and faiths
themselves. On some church-state questions, Reform Jews are on the opposite side from Orthodox Jews. In the Christian churches, liberals and
conservatives (or, as some would have it, modernists and traditionalists)
find themselves opposing one another across denominational lines, creating a new politics.

What sense can be made of this, and, in particular, of the turn toward
faith-based institutions? Is a new national consensus on church-state questions possible?

A consensus is possible—even if it will be hard to achieve—if the current arguments are understood as the third stage in a long national debate.

White Protestant hegemony in America—the first stage—began to
erode with the end of Prohibition, arguably the last political project to

unite mainline and fundamentalist Protestants. But the formal dominance of Protestantism was largely repealed in the 1960s, often with the strong support of progressive Protestants themselves.

The second stage involved a hard push for separation, including many of the relevant court decisions. It was no accident that this occurred as the country was coming to terms with its historic treatment of minorities. "I see the '60s as a time when we began to grow up a little bit," says Davis, director of the Baylor center. "If we want to be a democracy that supports the rights of minority groups, including religious minorities, we can't have a government that stands behind and supports one world view."

John F. Kennedy's election as president marked the full entry of Roman Catholics into the mainstream of American life. The civil rights movement sought to right historic wrongs done to African Americans. The era swept away long-standing barriers to Jews. It saw the effective end of restrictive covenants and the rise of new movements to defend the rights of Latinos and Asians. All brought the pervasively white and Protestant ethos in government-financed institutions and society into question.

Today's commotion is rooted in a new fear—that the combination of legal decisions and cultural trends has marginalized religion more than is either necessary for religious freedom or desirable for the country. In creating what Yale Law School Professor Stephen Carter called "The Culture of Disbelief," the country seemed to replace old prejudices (of race and religion) with a new prejudice against belief itself.[3]

The current renegotiation of boundaries—the third stage—has already borne fruit. In 1995 new federal guidelines to school administrators were designed to make clear that while the state cannot impose religion, students cannot be forced to be secular against their will or silenced in their personal expressions of religion. Individual students could not be stopped from praying, Jewish students could not be barred from wearing skull caps, any kid who wanted to talk about religion on school grounds had the right to do so. As the president said at the time, the Constitution "does not require children to leave their religion at the schoolhouse door."

In 1997 the administration issued guidelines requiring government supervisors to respect individual expressions of faith by religious employees. Christians, the guidelines said, can keep Bibles on their desks, Muslim women can wear head scarves, Jewish workers should be accommodated as much as possible in scheduling so they can honor the High Holidays. This may all seem like common sense, but it reflects an awareness that a desire to preserve religious freedom entails both keeping the government out of the way and protecting the free expression of believers.

The battle over expanded government aid to faith-based institutions will not be so easy. Rogers calls it "the wrong way to do right." She means that the admirable efforts by faith-based charities should get much more private and corporate support but not government help. Yet Gore's endorsement of what has come to be known as "charitable choice" suggests a slow shifting of the boundaries being drawn by moderate and even liberal Democrats who have come to see the churches as indispensable allies to government in solving problems.

The NAE's Cizik thinks the rise of religious feeling in America and a decline in the hostility to religious institutions may be a sign that "a new, more acceptable consensus would replace partisan religious fights." Even active participants in the culture wars, he says, are tired of them.

Amen to that. And if a new consensus still involves some contention, that's neither surprising or disappointing. What else would you expect in a country where people have rioted over the Ten Commandments? But precisely because every generation of Americans has been willing to argue about it, we have managed not only to preserve but also to expand religious liberty.

17

Supporting Black Churches
Faith, Outreach, and the Inner-City Poor

JOHN J. DIIULIO JR.

BLACK AMERICANS are in many ways the most religious people in America. Some 82 percent of blacks (versus 67 percent of whites) are church members; 82 percent of blacks (versus 55 percent of whites) say that religion is "very important in their life." Eighty-six percent of blacks (versus 60 percent of whites) believe that religion "can answer all or most of today's problems."[1]

And the religious faith of black Americans issues today, as it has for more than a century, in active work in the community. In his 1899 classic, *The Philadelphia Negro: A Social Study,* W. E. B. Du Bois observed, "Without wholly conscious effort the Negro church has become a centre of social intercourse to a degree unknown in white churches. . . . Consequently all movements for social betterment are apt to centre in the churches."[2] Almost 100 years later, in their 1990 *The Black Church in the African-American Experience,* Eric Lincoln and Lawrence Mamiya made a similar finding. In their surveys encompassing nearly 1,900 black ministers and more than 2,100 black churches, some 71 percent of black clergy reported that their churches engaged in community outreach programs. Urban churches, Lincoln and Mamiya found, were generally more engaged in outreach than rural ones. From their comprehensive survey, the authors concluded, "We suspect that black churches, on the whole, are more socially active in their communities than white churches and that they also tend to participate in a greater range of community programs."[3]

In my view, the most vital work of these active black churches is that done on the streets in America's inner cities. Day by day, clergy, volunteers, and people of faith monitor, mentor, and minister to the daily needs of the inner-city black children, who, through absolutely no fault of their own, live in neighborhoods where opportunities are few and drugs, crime, and failed public schools are common. There, faith-driven community activists strive against the odds to help these children—from innocent toddlers, to pregnant teenagers, to young men on probation—avoid violence, achieve literacy, gain jobs, and otherwise reach adulthood physically, educationally, and economically whole.

Is Religion the Answer?

Is there any social scientific evidence to show that religious do-gooding does any good or to justify the faith of most black Americans that religion can "answer all or most of today's problems"?

During the past several years, journalists have begun to take a keen interest in that question. In September 1996, the cover of *US News and World Report* asked, "Can Churches Cure America's Ills?" and the stories answered largely in the affirmative. A June 1998 *Newsweek* cover story on the inner-city ministry of Boston's Reverend Eugene Rivers III had been preceded by articles on Rivers's work by Joe Klein in the *New Yorker*, George Will in the *Washington Post*, and Bob Herbert in the *New York Times*. Another 1998 feature, this one in *Time* magazine, heralded Brother Bill, a Catholic lay worker who "repeatedly walks into gunfire to stop the shooting—and love the unloved."

While such "faith factor" journalism is out ahead of the empirical research on religion and social action, it is hardly pure hype. As UCLA's James Q. Wilson has succinctly summarized the small but not insignificant body of credible evidence to date, "Religion, independent of social class, reduces deviance." When criminologist Byron Johnson and medical research scientist David Larson reviewed some 400 juvenile delinquency studies published between 1980 and 1997, they found that the more scientific the study, the more optimistic its findings are about the extent to which "religion reduces deviance." A 1995 article in the journal *Criminology* by David Evans found that religion, "as indicated by religious activities, had direct personal effects on adult criminality as measured by a broad range of criminal acts:" [4]

In relation to black inner-city poverty and related social ills, perhaps the single most illustrative line of "religion reduces deviance" research begins with a 1985 study by Harvard economist Richard Freeman, runs through the work of Larson and Johnson, and continues through the community development, mentoring, and faith factor research of analysts at Public/Private Ventures, a Philadelphia-based national nonprofit youth policy research organization.

In 1985 Freeman reported that churchgoing, independent of other factors, made young black males from high-poverty neighborhoods substantially more likely to "escape" poverty, crime, and other social ills. In a reanalysis and extension of Freeman's work published by the Manhattan Institute, Larson and Johnson mine national time series data on urban black youth and find that, using a more multidimensional measure of religious commitment than churchgoing, religion is indeed a powerful predictor of escaping poverty, crime, and other social ills, more powerful even than such variables as peer influences. Like Freeman, Larson and Johnson conjecture that the potential of churchgoing and other religious influences to improve the life prospects of poor black urban youth is in part a function of how churchgoing and other faith factors influence how young people spend their time, the extent of their engagement in positive structured activities, and the degree to which they are supported by responsible adults. "Though more research is needed in this area," they conclude, there is "significant initial evidence that the African-American church may play a key role as an agency of local social control in communities often typified by disorder and disadvantage." [5]

This conjecture is borne out in part by a 1998 P/PV analysis, based on original survey and field research, of how predominantly minority low-income urban youth spend their time in the "moderately poor" neighborhoods of Austin, Texas; Savannah, Georgia; and St. Petersburg, Florida. First, the bad news. Researchers Cynthia L. Sipe and Patricia Ma found that a majority of children in three age groups—twelve to fourteen, fifteen to seventeen, and eighteen to twenty—in each neighborhood in each city spent most of their after-school time just "hanging out." Overall, "a disturbingly high share" (from 15 percent to 25 percent) were "not engaged in any positive structured activities," had "no or very few adults in their lives," and were "not working."[6] There is every reason to suppose that the unsupported fraction runs even higher in the poorest inner-city neighborhoods.

Now, however, the good news. Across all age groups and cities, most youth who did receive adult support and guidance (whether at home, in school, or in community organizations) and did participate in positive, structured activities were significantly more likely than their "disconnected" peers to succeed. Finally, the good news about religion. The P/PV study had expected to find that public schools and programs like Boys Clubs and Girls Clubs, Police Athletic League, Ys, and Big Brothers, Big Sisters provided substantial support for children in these communities. Those expectations were not entirely disappointed. But what the study also revealed was that churches and faith-based programs played a major "support for youth" role in providing after-school "safe havens," recreation, mentoring, child care, meals, and more. In the Savannah study site, for example, fifty-two churches dwarfed schools in sheer numbers and in outreach programs and activities for neighborhood youth, 97 percent of them black.

The unavoidable conclusion, notes P/PV's Gary Walker, a twenty-five-year veteran of the field, is, "Most private, nonprofit mentoring programs, like most social policy-driven youth development programs, simply don't reach or support the most severely at-risk inner-city youth."[7] Where secular mentoring and conventional social services programs for poor urban youth typically end, churches and religious outreach ministries often begin.

Black Church Outreach

The black church's uniquely powerful community outreach tradition is grounded in eight major historically black Christian churches: African Methodist Episcopal, African Methodist Episcopal Zion, Christian Methodist Episcopal, Church of God in Christ, National Baptist Convention of America, National Baptist Convention USA, National Missionary Baptist

Convention, and the Progressive National Baptist Convention. Besides the 65,000 churches and 20 million members of the eight denominations, scores of independent or quasi-independent black churches or church networks and at least nine certified religious training programs operated by accredited seminaries are also directed toward ministry in black churches and black faith communities.

Unfortunately, until recently, that outreach tradition and what it portends for social action against inner-city ills has been largely ignored by a strange bedfellows assortment of academics and intellectual elites.

Until the 1990s, for example, the richly religious lives of black Americans and the black church outreach tradition were given short shrift by both historians and social scientists, and not just by white historians and social scientists. Writing in 1994 in a special double edition of *National Journal of Sociology*, Andrew Billingsley, a dean of black family studies, noted that the subject was largely ignored even by leading black scholars who were keenly aware of "the social significance of the black church," including many who "were actually members of a black church."[8]

For example, James Blackwell's 1975 book *The Black Community*, considered by Billingsley and several other experts to be "the best study" of its kind since Du Bois's *The Philadelphia Negro,* devoted not a single chapter to the black church, and Billingsley's own 1968 *Black Families in White America,* written as a rebuttal to the 1965 Moynihan Report on the breakdown of the American black family, "devoted less than two pages to discussing the relevance of the black church as a support system for African-American families." Billingsley speculates that black intellectuals ignored black churches in part out of a false fidelity to the canons of objective scholarship.

A refined and empirically well-grounded perspective on variations in the extent of black church outreach is provided by sociologist Harold Dean Trulear, an ordained black minister who did outreach work in New Jersey, taught for eight years at the New York Theological Seminary, has conducted extensive research on black clergy training, and is now vice president for research on religion and at-risk youth at P/PV.[9]

"When it comes to youth and community outreach in the inner city," Trulear cautions, "not all black urban churches are created equal. . . . Inner-city churches with high resident membership cater more to high-risk neighborhood youth than . . . black churches with inner-city addresses but increasingly or predominantly suburbanized or commuting congregations. . . . It's the small and medium-sized churches . . . (especially) the so-called . . . blessing stations and specialized youth chapels with their charismatic leader and their small, dedicated staff of adult volunteers (that) . . . do a disproportionate amount of the up close and personal outreach work with the worst-off inner-city youth."

When it comes to social action against urban problems and the plight of the black inner-city poor, the reality is that black churches cannot do it all (or do it alone) and that not all black churches do it. But that reality should obscure neither the black church tradition nor its many and powerful contemporary manifestations from Boston to Austin, from New York to Los Angeles.

Today a number of intellectuals and policy leaders are reclaiming the black church tradition. In a 1997 essay in the *Brookings Review,* Boston University's Glenn Loury and Tufts University's Linda Datcher-Loury, writing not only as economists but as blacks attached to black churches, argued persuasively that voluntary associations, "as exemplified by religious institutions," can be valuable allies in the battle against social pathology. From a less academic, more practice-driven perspective, Robert L. Woodson, Sr., president of the National Center for Neighborhood Enterprise in Washington, D.C., reclaims that black church outreach tradition in his 1998 book, *The Triumphs of Joseph: How Today's Community Healers Are Reviving Our Streets and Neighborhoods.*[10]

The Least of Us, the Rest of Us

If black church outreach is so potent, then how come inner-city poverty, crime, and other problems remain so severe? That is a fair question, but it can easily be turned around: how much worse would things be in Boston and Jamaica Queens, Philadelphia and Los Angeles, and other cities were it not for the until recently largely unsung efforts of faith-based youth and community outreach efforts? How much more would government or other charitable organizations need to expend, and how many volunteers would suddenly need to be mobilized, in the absence of church-anchored outreach? The only defensible answers are "much worse" and "lots," respectively.

Religious institutions alone cannot reasonably be expected to cure the social problems that disproportionately afflict the black inner-city poor. It remains to be seen how, if at all, the local faith-based efforts can be taken to scale in ways that predictably, reliably, and cost effectively cut crime, reduce poverty, or yield other desirable social consequences.

But overlooking, unduly discounting, or simply failing to support the outreach efforts of black churches and other inner-city faith communities is the single biggest mistake that can be made by anyone who cares about the future of the truly disadvantaged men, women, and children of all races who call the inner cities home.

Citizens who for whatever reasons are nervous about religion or enhanced church-state partnerships should focus on the consistent finding that faith-based outreach efforts benefit poor unchurched neighborhood children most of all. If these churches are so willing to support and reach out to "the least of these," surely they deserve the human and financial support of the rest of us—corporations, foundations, other Christian churches, and, where appropriate, government agencies.

18

"No Aid to Religion?"
Charitable Choice and the First Amendment

RONALD J. SIDER AND
HEIDI ROLLAND UNRUH

As GOVERNMENT struggles to solve a confounding array of poverty-related social problems—deficient education, un- and underemployment, substance abuse, broken families, substandard housing, violent crime, inadequate health care, crumbling urban infrastructures—it has turned increasingly to the private sector, including a wide range of faith-based agencies. As described in Stephen Monsma's *When Sacred and Secular Mix*, public funding for nonprofit organizations with a religious affiliation is surprisingly high. Of the faith-based child service agencies Monsma surveyed, 63 percent reported that more than 20 percent of their budget came from public funds.[1]

Government's unusual openness to cooperation with the private religious sector arises in part from public disenchantment with its programs but also from an increasingly widespread view that the nation's acute social problems have moral and spiritual roots. Acknowledging that social problems arise both from unjust socioeconomic structures and from misguided personal choices, scholars, journalists, politicians, and community activists are calling attention to the vital and unique role that religious institutions play in social restoration.

Though analysis of the outcomes of faith-based social services is as yet incomplete, the available evidence suggests that some of those services may be more effective and cost-efficient than similar secular and government programs. One oft-cited example is Teen Challenge, the world's largest residential drug rehabilitation program, with a documented rehabilitation rate of 86 percent—a vastly higher success rate than most other programs, at a substantially lower cost. Multiple studies identify religion as a key variable in reducing health risk factors, keeping marriages together, and escaping the downward spiral of gangs, drugs, and prison that overwhelms many young, urban African-American males.

The New Cooperation and the Courts

The potential of public-private cooperative efforts involving religious agencies has been constrained by traditional First Amendment interpretation. The ruling interpretive principle on public funding of religious nonprofits— following the metaphor of the wall of separation between church and state, as set forth in *Everson* v. *Board of Education* (1947)—has been "no aid to religion." While most court cases have involved funding for religious elementary and secondary schools, clear implications have been drawn for other types of "pervasively sectarian" organizations. A religiously affiliated institution may receive public funds—but only if it is not too religious.

Application of the no-aid policy by the courts, however, has been confusing. The Supreme Court has provided no single, decisive definition of "pervasively sectarian" to determine which institutions qualify for public funding, and judicial tests have been applied inconsistently. Rulings attempting to separate the sacred and secular aspects of religiously based programs often appear arbitrary from a faith perspective and at worst border on impermissible entanglement. As a result of this legal confusion, some agencies receiving public funds pray openly with their clients, while other agencies have been banned even from displaying religious symbols. Faith-based child welfare agencies have greater freedom in incorporating religious components than religious schools working with the same population. Only a few publicly funded religious agencies have been challenged in the courts, but such leniency may not continue. The lack of legal recourse leaves agencies vulnerable to pressures from public officials and community leaders to secularize their programs.

The Supreme Court's restrictive rulings on aid to religious agencies stand in tension with the government's movement toward greater reliance on private sector social initiatives. If the no-aid principle were applied consistently against all religious agencies now receiving public funding—such as churches with government-funded food programs or day care agencies—government provision of social services would face significant setbacks. This ambiguous state of affairs for public-private cooperation has created a climate of mistrust and misunderstanding, in which faith-based agencies are reluctant to expose themselves to risk of lawsuits, civic authorities are confused about what is permissible, and multiple pressures push religious organizations into hiding or compromising their identity, while at the same time many public officials and legislators are willing to look the other way when effective faith-based social service programs include religious content.

Fortunately, an alternative principle of First Amendment interpretation, which Monsma identifies as the "equal treatment" strain, has been emerging in the Supreme Court. This line of reasoning—as in *Widmar* v. *Vincent* (1981) and *Rosenberger* v. *Rector* (1995)—holds that public access to facilities or benefits cannot exclude religious groups. Although the principle has not yet been applied to funding for social service agencies, it could be a precedent for defending cooperation between government and faith-based agencies where the offer of funding is available to any qualifying agency.

The section of the 1996 welfare reform law known as Charitable Choice paves the way for this cooperation by prohibiting government from discriminating against nonprofit applicants for certain types of social service funding (whether by grant, contract, or voucher) on the basis of their religious nature. Charitable Choice also shields faith-based agencies receiving federal funding from governmental pressures to alter their religious character—among other things, ensuring their freedom to display religious symbols and to hire staff who share their religious perspective. Charitable Choice prohibits religious nonprofits from using government funds for "inherently religious" activities defined as "sectarian worship, instruction, or proselytization"—but allows them to raise money from nongovernment sources to cover the costs of any such activities they choose to integrate into their program. Clearly, Charitable Choice departs from the dominant "pervasively sectarian" standard for determining eligibility for government funding, which has restricted the funding of thoroughly religious organizations. It makes religiosity irrelevant to the selection of agencies for public-private cooperative ventures and emphasizes instead the public goods to be achieved by cooperation. At the same time, Charitable Choice protects clients' First Amendment rights by ensuring that services are not conditional on religious preference, that client participation in religious activities is voluntary, and that an alternative nonreligious service provider is available.

The First Amendment and the Case for Charitable Choice

Does Charitable Choice violate the First Amendment's nonestablishment and free exercise clauses? We think not. As long as participants in faith-based programs freely choose those programs over a "secular" provider and may opt out of particular religious activities within the program, no one is coerced to participate in religious activity, and freedom of religion is preserved. As long as government is equally open to funding programs rooted in any religious perspective—whether Islam, Christianity, philosophic naturalism, or no explicit faith perspective—government is not establishing or providing preferential benefits to any specific religion or to religion in general. As long as religious institutions maintain autonomy over such crucial areas as program content and staffing, the integrity of their identity and mission is maintained. As long as agencies are required to account for grant and contract funds in accordance with the ban on expenditures for inherently religious activities, no taxpayer need fear that taxes are paying for religion. While Charitable Choice may increase interactions between government and religious institutions, these interactions do not in themselves violate the First Amendment. Charitable Choice is designed precisely to discourage such interactions from leading to impermissible entanglement or establishment of religion.

Not only does Charitable Choice not violate proper church-state relations, it strengthens First Amendment protections. In the current context of extensive government funding for a wide array of social services, limiting government funds to allegedly "secular" programs actually offers preferential treatment to one specific religious worldview.

In setting forth this argument, we distinguish four types of social service providers. First are secular providers who make no explicit reference to God or any ultimate values. People of faith may work in such an agency—say, a job training program that teaches job skills and work habits—but staff use only current techniques from the social and medical sciences without reference to religious faith. Expressing explicit faith commitments of any sort is considered inappropriate.

Second are religiously affiliated providers (of any religion) who incorporate little inherently religious programming and rely primarily on the same medical and social science methods as a secular agency. Such a program may be historically rooted in a faith community; a staff with strong theological reasons for their involvement; religious symbols may be present. A religiously affiliated job training program might be housed in a church, and clients might be informed about the church's religious programs and about the availability of a chaplain's services. But the content of the training curriculum would be very similar to that of a secular program.

Third are exclusively faith-based providers whose programs rely on inherently religious activities, making little or no use of techniques from the medical and social sciences. An example would be a prayer support group and seminar on biblical principles of work for job seekers.

Fourth are holistic faith-based providers who combine techniques from the medical and social sciences with inherently religious components such as prayer, worship, and the study of sacred texts. A holistic job training program might incorporate explicitly biblical principles into a curriculum that teaches job skills and work habits and invite clients to pray with program staff.

Everyone agrees that public funding of only the last two types of providers would constitute government establishment of religion. But if government (because of the "no aid to religion" principle) funds only secular programs, is this a properly neutral policy?

Not really, for two reasons. First, given the widespread public funding for private social services, if government funds only secular programs, it puts all faith-based programs at a disadvantage. Government would tax everyone—both religious and secular—and then fund only allegedly secular programs. Government-run or government-funded programs would be competing in the same fields with faith-based programs lacking access to such support.

Second, secular programs are not religiously neutral. Implicitly, purely "secular" programs convey the message that nonreligious technical knowledge and skills are sufficient to address social problems such as low job skills and single parenthood. Implicitly, they teach the irrelevance of a spiritual dimension to human life. Although secular programs may not explicitly uphold the tenets of philosophical naturalism and the belief that nothing exists except the natural order, implicitly they support such a worldview. Rather than being religiously neutral, "secular" programs implicitly convey a set of naturalistic beliefs about the nature of persons and ultimate reality that serve the same function as religion. Vast public funding of only secular programs means government bias in favor of one particular quasi-religious perspective, namely, philosophical naturalism.

The fact that religiously affiliated agencies (type two) have received large amounts of funding in spite of the "no aid to religion" principle poses another problem. These agencies often claim a clear religious identity—in the agency's history or name, in the religious identity and motivations of sponsors and some staff, in the provision of a chaplain, or in visible religious symbols. By choice or in response to external pressures, however, little in their program content and methods distinguishes many of these agencies from their fully secular counterparts. Prayer, spiritual counseling, Bible studies, and invitations to join a faith community are not featured; in fact, most such agencies would consider inherently religious activities inappropriate to social service programs.

Millions of public dollars have gone to support the social service programs of religiously affiliated agencies. There are three possible ways to understand this apparent potential conflict with the "no aid to religion" principle. Perhaps these agencies are finally only nominally religious, and in fact are essentially secular institutions, in which case their religious sponsors should be raising questions. Or perhaps they are more pervasively religious than they have appeared to government funders, in which case the government should have withheld funding.

Proselytizing

RONALD SIDER AND HEIDI ROLLAND UNRUH

In debates sparked by Charitable Choice, the issue of religious proselytizing often takes center stage. The possibility that government-funded faith-based organizations would incorporate evangelistic elements into social programs raises important ethical, theological, legal, and pragmatic questions. Does proselytizing inherently entail some measure of coercion, particularly when clients are in the vulnerable position of needing aid from the service agency? Do faith-based groups provide services because they care about the clients or as an inducement for clients to join their church or faith group? Does an evangelistic component in a government-funded program inevitably infringe on the religious rights of clients or violate church-state separation? On the other hand, will the receipt of public funding bridle the efforts of evangelistically oriented faith-based organizations to nurture faith in those they serve, and how would this affect the character and outcomes of their service?

Responsibly addressing these questions calls for continued careful research on how faith-based organizations respond to Charitable Choice, including a specific focus on the religious components of their programs. Without this factual foundation, the discussion of proselytizing too easily becomes captive to hopes, fears, or stereotypes about evangelistic religious groups. Four key questions must be raised:

—How much evangelism takes place?

—What kind of evangelism takes place, and how is it integrated into the social service?

—What is the impact of the evangelism?

—Why do faith-based organizations evangelize?

According to Charitable Choice, "No funds provided directly to institutions or organizations to provide services and administer programs under [the

The third explanation may be that these agencies are operating with a specific, widely accepted worldview that holds that people may need God for their spiritual well-being, but that their social problems can be addressed exclusively through medical and social science methods. Spiritual nurture,

Charitable Choice provision] shall be expended for sectarian worship, instruc-tion, or proselytization." Clarification of the terms "sectarian worship, instruc-tion, or proselytization" will be important to the ongoing implementation of Charitable Choice, as the terms have different meanings to different groups.

The restriction against use of funds for religious activities does not apply in the case of voucher funding. Nor does Charitable Choice explicitly forbid faith-based groups with state contracts or grants to use private funds to conduct in-herently religious activities in the context of social service programs funded by government. Service recipients retain the right, however, to opt out of religious activities or to receive their benefits from a nonreligious provider, and no faith-based organization receiving public funds may discriminate on the basis of faith in providing services.

With these safeguards, proselytizing does not represent an insurmountable obstacle to the effective, ethical, and constitutional implementation of Chari-table Choice. It is possible for faith-based groups funded by government to strike a balance between respect for the First Amendment and care for the spiri-tual needs of clients. Some such groups view the spiritual component of their social ministry as integral to their effectiveness, as well as to their mission. Many are nurturing the faith of clients in ways that are privately funded, voluntary, noncoercive, and respectful of religious pluralism—that is, in ways that would not be affected by receipt of public funds.

Although concerns about proselytizing must be taken seriously, the best interests of church, state, and community are served when there is room at the Charitable Choice table for holistic programs that include sharing faith with program participants—as long as these religious components are voluntary and supported exclusively with private funds.

in this worldview, is important in its place but has no direct bearing on achieving public goods like drug rehabilitation or overcoming welfare de-pendency. Such a worldview acknowledges the spiritual dimension of per-sons and the existence of a transcendent realm outside of nature. But it also teaches (whether explicitly or implicitly) a particular understanding of God and persons, by addressing people's social needs independently of their spiritual nature. By allowing aid to flow only to the religiously affiliated agencies holding this understanding, government in effect has given preferential treatment to a particular religious worldview.

Holistic faith-based agencies (type four), however, operate on the belief that no area of a person's life, whether psychological, physical, social, or economic, can be adequately addressed in isolation from the spiritual. Agencies operating out of this worldview consider the explicitly spiritual components of their programs—used in conjunction with conventional, secular social service methods—as fundamental to their ability to achieve the secular social goals desired by government. Government has in the past considered such agencies ineligible for public funding, though they may provide the same services as their religiously affiliated counterparts.

Some claim that channeling public funds through a holistic religious program threatens the First Amendment, while funding religiously affiliated agencies does not. To the contrary, the pervasively sectarian standard has also constituted a genuine, though more subtle, establishment of religion, because it supports one type of religious worldview while penalizing holistic beliefs. It should not be the place of government to judge between religious worldviews, but this is what the no-aid principle has required the courts to do. Selective religious perspectives on the administration of social services are deemed permissible for government to aid. Those who believe that explicitly religious content does not play a central role in addressing social problems are free to act on this belief with government support; those who believe that spiritual nurture is an integral aspect of social transformation are not.

The alternative is to pursue a policy that discriminates neither against nor in favor of any religious perspective. Charitable Choice enables the government to offer equal access to benefits to any faith-based nonprofit, as long as the money is not used for inherently religious activities and the agency provides the social benefits desired by government. Charitable Choice does not ask governmental bodies to decide which agencies are too religious. It clearly indicates the types of "inherently religious" activities that are off limits for government funding. The government must continue to make choices about which faith-based agencies will receive funds, but eligibility for funding is to be based on an agency's ability to provide specific public goods, rather than on its religious character. Charitable Choice moves the focus of church-state interactions away from the religious beliefs and practices of social service agencies and onto the common goals of helping the poor and strengthening the fabric of public life.

A Model for Change

Our treasured heritage of religious freedom demands caution as we contemplate new forms of church-state cooperation, but caution does not preclude change if the benefits promise to outweigh the dangers. Indeed, change is required if the pervasively sectarian standard is actually biased in favor of some religious perspectives and against others.

For church and state to cooperate successfully, both must remain true to their roles and mission. Religious organizations must refrain from accepting public funds if that means compromising their beliefs and undermining their effectiveness and integrity. Fortunately, Charitable Choice allows faith-based agencies to maintain their religious identity while expanding the possibilities for constructive cooperation between church and state in addressing the nation's most serious social problems.

19

The Wrong Way to Do Right
A Challenge to Charitable Choice

MELISSA ROGERS

THE 2000 presidential election has reinvigorated a very old debate—what is required of a nation for religious freedom to prosper? Presidential candidates Governor George W. Bush and Vice President Al Gore are encouraging new partnerships between faith-based organizations and the government to solve pressing social problems. Without question, their goals are laudable—religion should play a greater role in improving the lives of the less fortunate. But their proposals would needlessly sacrifice a measure of religious freedom.

Both candidates' proposals arise from the "charitable choice" provision first made law as part of the massive overhaul of the welfare system in 1996. That provision popularized the term "faith-based organization" and proposed a dramatic revision of the law of church and state.

Before 1996, instead of being known as faith-based organizations, religious organizations generally were known by one of two labels drawn from court decisions. A religiously affiliated entity is a group that has ties to religion but is set up to perform secular social services. These groups, such as Catholic Charities and Lutheran Services in America, have long received public funding. A "pervasively sectarian" organization, on the other hand, is a term the Supreme Court has used to refer to "an institution in which religion is so pervasive that a substantial portion of its functions are subsumed in a religious mission."[1] Pervasively religious groups would include, for example, houses of worship or a drug rehabilitation ministry that relies on acceptance of the gospel in its treatment program. While the Supreme Court has ruled that religiously affiliated entities may receive tax funds, the Court generally has barred the flow of tax funds to pervasively religious organizations.

Why has the Supreme Court traditionally refused to permit tax funds to flow to pervasively religious organizations like churches? Because religion pervades these entities, public funding for any part of them becomes unconstitutionally advancing religion itself. In a 1988 case the Court specifically warned against allowing tax funds to flow to pervasively religious social service organizations. Justice Rehnquist, writing for the Court, observed, "There is a risk that direct government funding, even if it is designated for specific secular purposes, may nonetheless advance the pervasively sectarian institution's 'religious mission.'"[2] The Court also has noted that, to the extent the government attempts to separate sacred from secular in an entity like a church, it risks becoming excessively entangled with religion, which also violates the Constitution.

Charitable choice, however, attempts to obliterate any legal distinction between religiously affiliated and pervasively religious organizations, allowing both to receive tax funds. As governor, George W. Bush signed an executive order urging state agencies to use the charitable choice provision of the welfare reform law. Bush commented that "for too long government has excluded churches and synagogues from the delivery of welfare."[3] In his presidential campaign, Bush has called for "making 'charitable choice' explicitly applicable to all federal laws that authorize the government to use non-governmental entities to provide services to beneficiaries with federal dollars," and has pledged to remove all barriers to the use of federal funds by faith-based groups.[4] Vice President Gore has also explicitly embraced the charitable choice concept and called for its extension.[5]

The presidential candidates' endorsements of these schemes, however, don't make them constitutional or advisable. By allowing tax funds to flow to churches and other pervasively religious entities, charitable choice allows the state to advance religion and risks excessive church-state entanglement. And, contrary to the claims of charitable choice proponents, recent

Supreme Court rulings allowing some discrete, government-provided educational aids for students at public, private, and parochial schools don't
come close to constitutionalizing these schemes. Further, charitable choice
creates other clear risks for religion and religious liberty.

Two things are often lacking in the debate on this issue. One is an
examination of the dangers these new partnerships create for churches and
other prevasively religious groups. The other is consideration of some al-
ternatives for boosting religion's role in the delivery of social services. Charitable choice is neither the best nor the only way for religious organizations
to serve the less fortunate.

One immutable consequence of receiving tax funds is that regulation
goes along with it. The government will regulate tax-subsidized social service providers, even if they are houses of worship. Some regulation is specified in the charitable choice provision itself. For example, the charitable
choice provision requires providers (including churches and other religious
missions) to submit to an audit. Charitable choice providers also must
refrain from using contract money for "sectarian worship, instruction or
proselytization."[6] Vice President Gore has articulated what appears to be a
similar "safeguard," insisting that the government "must continue to prohibit direct proselytizing as part of any publicly funded efforts."[7]

Proponents of these schemes have not begun to explain how such safeguards would be implemented. How will the government define "direct
proselytizing," much less ensure that a church isn't using public money to
do it? Adequate enforcement of this safeguard in a church or like institution will put it on a collision course with the constitutional prohibition
against excessive church-state entanglements. On the other side of the coin,
how will the government fund programs that are successful precisely because of their religious content without resulting in unconstitutional state
support for religion itself?

The regulation specified in charitable choice, however, is clearly the
floor rather than the ceiling of relevant regulation for tax-funded religious
ministries. Other regulation generally follows tax money. Even though religious ministries will likely agree with the goals of these laws, proving
compliance with it by filing annual compliance reports, waiving rights of
confidentiality, and submitting to governmental investigations may take a

large toll on religious autonomy. And one news report of fraud by some rogue group, claiming to be a church, will lead to tighter restrictions.

Proponents of tax-subsidized church ministries correctly point out that they have taken steps to try to preserve religious organizations' independence. Vice President Gore insists that faith-based organizations can perform their social service "*with* public funds—and without having to alter the religious character that is so often the key to their effectiveness."[8] The charitable choice provision states that the religious organizations that receive tax funds will nevertheless retain "control over the definition, development, practice and expression of its religious beliefs."[9] Governor Bush promises that he will go even farther to try to free tax-subsidized, faith-based organizations from regulation.

Religious ministries, however, have reason to be wary. It is far from clear that the protections for religious social service providers that are part of charitable choice will withstand judicial scrutiny or be interpreted in ways that won't diminish religious autonomy. Indeed, a charitable choice proponent, Representative Nancy Johnson (R-Conn.), recently admitted: "Yes, there will be red tape. Churches who choose to receive Federal money will be regulated. If they do not like it, I cannot help it. If there are Federal dollars, you are accountable."[10]

And, of course, litigation often follows regulation. There are likely to be multiple legal challenges based on the applicable regulation as well as the constitutionality of various aspects of the law. In 1989, for example, one court refused to allow the Salvation Army to fire an employee who was a Wiccan because the employee's salary was paid substantially with tax money.[11] And a lawsuit has recently been filed against a tax-subsidized Baptist children's home because it fired an employee when it learned she was a lesbian.[12] How will these cases square with the charitable choice provision that attempts to allow tax-subsidized religious providers to discriminate on the basis of religion in hiring? Time-consuming litigation will tell.

Another danger of tax-funded religious ministries is the prospect that churches and other religious ministries could come to be viewed as administrative centers of government benefits and services. This could require houses of worship to terminate certain benefits, report on individuals, and otherwise police the system. Nothing could be farther from the church's historic identity as sanctuary. Moreover, other core elements of government programs may directly conflict with religious doctrine. The new welfare law's heavy emphasis on personal responsibility rather than communal sharing of burdens is contrary to some biblical precepts. And some religious persons may be torn between their own religious-based conviction that mothers of young children should stay at home and the welfare law's insistence that welfare mothers enter the job force.

Participation in these new partnerships also will diminish religion's prophetic witness, which sometimes includes the obligation to criticize those in power. It should come as no surprise when recipients of government subsidies are hesitant to criticize those who are paying the bills.

These new partnerships further threaten to drag religion into the political process of governmental appropriations. If lawmaking is like sausage-making, then the appropriations process is akin to the production of the cheapest, most questionable sausage in town. Religion enters this political fray at its peril. There is simply not enough tax money to fund every religious group in this country. Thus, the government will have to pick and choose when it awards grants and contracts. Elected officials will find it almost impossible to resist playing politics with religion. Houses of worship may compete against one another for government contracts, and, all too often, only majority faiths will prevail. While the government cannot heal all of the religious divisions in our country, it should not be in the business of driving us farther apart. As our founders recognized, passing out government tax money to churches will do just that.

Other serious implementation problems remain. How do we ensure, for example, that welfare beneficiaries will truly have the ability to reject religious options, especially when the charitable choice provision of the welfare reform law does not even require that beneficiaries be given notice that they have the right to a secular alternative? Churches should be concerned not only about their own autonomy but also about religious freedom and justice for all.

Can religious organizations simply refuse government funding if it begins to harm their ministries? Theoretically, yes. But once the new building is constructed and the program is expanded, it will be difficult to wean oneself from tax funding. Moreover, the risk of tax-subsidized church ministries isn't limited to the individual recipient of the funds. Allowing tax funds to flow to houses of worship creates a dangerous, far-reaching precedent. It flies in the face of our nation's historic recognition that religion is different and must be treated differently in many circumstances. Religion is subject to special limitations at times (for example, pervasively religious institutions like churches may not receive tax funding), and at times religion enjoys special accommodations from the government (for example, religious organizations may discriminate on the basis of religion in hiring). These principles are the yin and yang of religious freedom, ensuring a healthy separation of the institutions of church and state, which affords each maximum freedom to pursue its distinct agenda.

Upsetting this balance will have serious consequences. Asking the government to treat churches the same as everything else in the area of tax-funded social services (to fund houses of worship like everything else) will come back to haunt us in other areas. Ultimately, it will undercut a wide range of protections for religion from government.

For all these reasons, we should be extremely careful about financial partnerships between the government and religious organizations. Instead of racing to tack charitable choice to every stream of federal and state social service funding, legislators should study how charitable choice is being implemented already. Instead of assuming that religion and religious liberty will be strengthened by providing tax subsidies to houses of worship and other pervasively religious groups, legislators ought to call hearings to explore the profound constitutional dangers and policy concerns raised by charitable choice. And, instead of allowing charitable choice to monopolize the discussion regarding church-state cooperation in the provision of social services, legislators and policymakers ought to explore the many other ways in which religious institutions and government may cooperate. While charitable choice is the wrong way to do right, there are many right ways for church and state to do right together.

Of course, the government should maintain a strong safety net for those in need—in today's society, religious and other private organizations cannot be expected to shoulder this burden alone. But church and state may work cooperatively in several ways.

First, legislatures should pass bills that provide enhanced tax incentives for charitable giving. This money could then be directed by individual taxpayers to the charities (including houses of worship) of their choice with no regulatory strings attached. Congress is currently considering the Charitable Giving Tax Relief Act (H.R. 1310), which would increase charitable giving by approximately $3 billion a year by allowing nonitemizers to deduct 50 percent of their charitable contributions over $500 annually. The Clinton administration and Governor Bush have endorsed this concept. Additional private funding for the programs of houses of worship may come from denominational appeals, charitable foundation grants, or even corporate sponsorships. Vice President Gore's idea of encouraging corporate matching funds for employees' gifts to religious organizations also is a laudable one.

Second, houses of worship and governmental officials should share information about needs and programs. Many houses of worship are uniquely situated to understand the community around them and to serve as incubators and motivators for an array of helpful social service projects. We can and should capitalize on these strengths without setting up new pipelines between federal and state treasuries and church coffers. The government may publicize the good work that private religious and other social service groups are doing and make referrals to these groups when appropriate.

Third, churches may choose to play a cooperative role with the state in certain volunteer programs. Along with other community groups, for example, religious institutions may participate in government-organized, volunteer mentoring projects as long as the government does not promote religion.

Fourth, houses of worship and other pervasively religious entities that haven't already done so should consider spinning off separate affiliates that are not thoroughly religious. Tax funding for these religiously affiliated entities is uncontroversial from a constitutional standpoint. Organizations that enter into these arrangements should realize that they will have to play by the rules that apply to other tax-funded social service providers. They should use tax money for secular services, not for religious activities. Catholic Charities and Lutheran Services in America have been doing this work for years.

These are just a few of the ways in which church and state may cooperate without creating funding ties that bind.

In his speech on the role of faith-based organizations, Vice President Gore caricatured the tensions underlying this issue. He said that "national leaders have been trapped in a dead-end debate" between "false choices: hollow secularism or right-wing religion."[13]

This rhetoric buys into an old saw that is widespread, convenient, and dead wrong. "Hollow secularists" aren't the only ones concerned about scrupulously maintaining the boundaries between the institutions of church and state. Many people of faith urge enforcement of these boundaries precisely because they value religion and religious freedom so much.

Respecting these boundaries does not mean that religion and politics don't mix. It does not mean church and state can't cooperate. It does not require reflexive resistance to new ideas on the church-state landscape. But respecting church-state boundaries does require resisting proposals that seriously and unnecessarily threaten the foundations of religious liberty in this country.

Our country is the most religiously vibrant in the world. This is no accident. Unlike so many other nations, religion in America relies on voluntary gifts, rather than compulsory tax funds. Unlike religion abroad, religion in this country is largely free from government direction and regulation. Charitable choice would undercut these foundations, causing religious freedom to suffer.

We must fight hopelessness and poverty. We can and should do so without sacrificing religious liberty.

20

What's an FBO?

JIM WALLIS

FBOS ARE "hot" these days. The emergence of the term "faith-based organizations" (and its acronym FBO) as a topic of discussion in the media, in academia, and on the campaign trail may signal one of the most significant new developments in American political and religious life. As an inner-city pastor friend recently said to me, "We've been discovered!" Faith-based organizations have been the mainstay of social service in this country for a long time—why the sudden new interest from the larger society?

Partly it's a result of the 1996 welfare reform legislation. As the federal government ended a direct role in many welfare programs, states and local communities came to the fore. And many of the most visible and effective programs in most communities are those that are faith based. Some have been there for a long time, many others were created in response to the new need.

Two of the most powerful forces in the country today are service and spirituality. The growing evidence of both is visible almost everywhere, and together they provide the most potent combination for changing our communities. They are growing streams of committed energy, which, as they begin to flow together, are creating a mighty river of action.

The recognition of this fact by the leading presidential candidates has raised the issue to a new level.

Vice President Al Gore, in May 1999, delivered a major policy speech in which he spoke of the "transformative power of faith-based approaches" in finding real solutions to the poverty and violence in local communities around the country. Then he went on to say that this role should be strategic, "not to be merely a shining anecdote in a pretty story told by a politician, but to have a seat at the national table when decisions get made."[1]

Two months later, on July 22, 1999, Governor George W. Bush outlined his position by saying, "In every instance where my administration sees a responsibility to help people, we will look first to faith-based organizations, charities, and community groups that have shown their ability to save and change lives." He also recognized that "there are some things the government should be doing..." and that government "must act in the common good—and that good is not common until it is shared by those in need."[2]

And Senator Bill Bradley, Gore's Democratic primary challenger, has long advocated a stronger role for the organizations of "civil society," including churches and religious organizations.

How the churches and FBOs respond to this new political interest will be a test of *our* faith and work. We must ensure that the political interest does go beyond pretty stories told by politicians using our language to a real working partnership. The interest of the politicians gives us an important opportunity to put the agenda of people in poverty on the political agenda. The well-being of the widow, fatherless, poor, and oppressed are subjects of constant discussion in the Bible. Making them a matter of serious political discussion in America today should be the mission of faith-based organizations.

Faith-based groups have an advantage over many other institutions when it comes to the kind of community organizing and development most needed today. It finally comes down to the question of social leadership—who is best situated to offer critical components like vision, direction, credibility, longevity, trust, and, of course, organizable constituencies. Faith communities may be in the best position to lead in efforts for social renewal because of their inherent characteristics and commitments, enabling them to be community conveners in broad-based efforts involving many different kinds of organizations. There are three sets of "essential ingredients" that are at the heart of why it is so critical to tap the power of faith communities.

—Message and Motivation. In a society where "market values" increasingly predominate, faith communities can offer a sense of meaning, purpose, and moral value that is increasingly missing in the society. When people feel reduced to mere consumers and life is reduced to shopping, faith communities can speak directly to the deep spiritual hunger that so many people experience. In the community of faith, persons are more than marketing data for advertisers or polling data for politicians; they are the children of God with immense and sacred value, created in the very image of God who gives a reason for being that far transcends "the bottom line."

Faith communities are also best situated to speak to the moral and spiritual impoverishment of the society that others seem to accept as inevitable. They can re-establish a sense of ethics and values when that is most necessary. The faith community makes it possible to do more than just "look out for number one." Faith communities offer people the practical opportunities to love their neighbor, serve their community, contribute to a larger purpose, and sacrifice for something worth believing in. In the community of faith, values of compassion, community, and solidarity have a theological foundation and not merely a sentimental one. Hope is more than an optimistic feeling; it is a firm conclusion drawn from trusting the promises of God.

The values you need for organizing are rooted in the very essence of the faith community. Eugene Rivers, pastor of the Azuza Christian Community in Boston, says that "only the church has the moral authority and the vocabulary to introduce transcendent concepts of personal worth and the sacredness of life that will both inspire responsibility on a personal level and introduce purpose and definition to the role of civil government on a societal level."[3] Thus, faith can be used to undergird, legitimize, and inspire social action.

—Counterculture and Prophetic Voice. Faith communities are intended to be distinct communities, with distinct ethics from the surrounding society. The apostle Paul writing to the Romans says, "Do not be conformed to this world, but be transformed by the renewing of your minds." Alternative visions arise from alternative communities. Such communities can become support bases for both nurturing and training, networking and mobilizing. The symbols and rituals of the faith community can become powerful educators and mobilizers for committed and even risky action. For example, black churches in the South constituted a coherent subculture in the midst of a white-dominated society. As such they reminded their members both of who they really were and what they could really do. Churches became the practical place to organize car-pools to sustain a bus boycott and the spiritual place to prepare oneself for nonviolent confrontation with police clubs and dogs.

A countercultural community can have a prophetic public voice. Here is where the authority and trust religious communities often enjoy in our society can be utilized for the common good. Who will tell the truth or even try to find it when falsehoods prevail? Who will stand up for those who are being left out and behind or whose human rights are being violated? Who will question the easy and hedonistic assumptions of the popular culture? The faith community has the moral authority to make justice a priority.

—Institution and Constituency. The most common institutions in local communities are the churches and the schools—and the churches are in much better shape. Churches have budgets, buildings, several kinds of meeting spaces, kitchens, nurseries, bathrooms, and parking lots—all of which are fundamental assets needed for organizing. They also have staffs, a cadre of professionally trained leadership, ties to larger denominational structures with greater resources, and a widely trusted historical tradition to build upon. Churches are the most commonly found institution in every kind of neighborhood, across all geographic, racial, cultural, and class boundaries. In some poor communities, churches are virtually the last standing institution. In those situations, it is often only the churches that have both the moral authority and institutional presence to lead efforts for civic reconstruction. With proximity to the problems, churches can work from the bottom up, redeeming kids one by one, claiming whole blocks and neighborhoods for transformation, calling for moral, civic, and political renewal in the broader community, city, and nation.

And, of course, the churches have a constituency. They actually have members—another prerequisite for organizing—who can be mobilized and brought together. The very nature of a universal membership in the faith community can be instrumental in helping to overcome the divisions between people, which are the greatest obstacle to organizing. And members of faith communities can be motivated to act on more than just their own self-interest but rather on the basis of the deeply held spiritual and moral values that undergird their faith. That faith can provide the kind of staying power so critically needed for long-term campaigns. Religious institutions, as well, have enduring power, as opposed to some other community institutions, which are often here today and gone tomorrow. Most churches plan to be a part of their communities for a very long time and, therefore, have a vested interest in their well-being.

Finally, because churches are built on relationships, they can provide a strong base for the kind of relational organizing style that is proving so effective around the country. Community organizer and sociologist Marshall Ganz speaks of this as a "covenantal" organizing style. He contrasts it with "issue based organizing," which is more "contractual," says Ganz. "It has a limited, short term, outcome based focus; often brings people into coalitions that dissolve immediately after the objective is attained, or isn't." Ganz prefers "interest based organizing," which is "covenantal." It has a longer-term focus of "identifying and developing those common interests which are affected by a variety of issues which come and go," he says. "Interest based organizing places a greater emphasis on building relationships as a way both to discern interests as well as to construct new interests which only emerge in the context of new relationship."[4]

A new "spiritual politics" and "social leadership" from the faith community is forging new solutions in local communities across the country by developing new civic partnerships committed not only to alleviating the effects of poverty but to overcoming it. Exciting and effective new partnerships are being initiated between many sectors.

First, the churches are getting their own house in order by coming together themselves across the political and theological spectrum to work on the vital task of welfare reform and the deeper agenda of overcoming poverty. A national "Christian Roundtable on Poverty and Welfare Reform," convened by Call to Renewal, has been meeting for three years, and local "roundtables" are forming around the country. Conservative Evangelicals are working alongside Catholic, black, and mainline Protestant churches. Together they are reading and putting into practice what the

Bible says about God's concern for the poor. In February 1999, nearly 500 of those faith-based organizations from more than forty states and twenty-nine denominations gathered at a Call to Renewal "National Summit on the Churches and Welfare Reform" in Washington, D.C., to pool resources, share best practices, and work toward a common agenda.

Churches and governments are developing new strategies to strengthen and empower nonprofits (including religious ones) to play a central role in delivering social services, without either weakening the First Amendment or weakening the religious component that makes faith-based organizations so effective. A public policy that recognizes and even funds the successful programs of both religious and secular nonprofits while respecting the separation of church and state is now critical.

Local businesses are combining to provide jobs and job training, microenterprise training centers, support in developing business and marketing plans, and changing restrictive financial policies to open the door to capital formation for new people and projects. The churches are an important partner in all of these efforts to provide the links into poor communities and to identify the people and projects most likely to succeed in new economic activities. Local congregations and their members are also playing a critical support role in mentoring programs to "walk with" people moving from welfare to work. Church-based child care and after-school programs are also playing a supportive role.

The devolution of national social policy to the local level has led politicians and social policy analysts to search for new answers, which is leading them to faith-based organizations. Vice President Gore proposed: "Let us put the solutions that faith-based organizations are pioneering at the very heart of our strategy for building a better, more just nation," and promised that if elected president, "the voices of faith-based organizations will be integral to the policies in my administration." And Governor Bush noted that "Government cannot be replaced by charities—but it can welcome them as partners, not resent them as rivals," and pledged "more support and resources—both private and public."

If faith-based organizations are indeed "invited to the table," our role will not simply be to make government more efficient but to make America more just. It will not just be to "clean up the mess" created by bad social policy or to take the place of legitimate government responsibilities but to bring a morally prophetic voice for new policies.

In this partnership, we will raise the common moral values on which our society must build and insist on a strong standard of the common good to guide public policy. We will argue that the development of public policy must not be merely dictated by the clash of power and competing interests but also by fundamental questions of right and wrong. The development of public policy must be shaped by asking what our moral vision is, what kind of people we want to be, and what kind of country we want to have.

For example, today there is an incredibly vibrant "direct citizen" politics occurring in local communities. Much of it is tied to nonprofit institutions, among them many faith-based organizations. National politics must wake up to that and begin to connect with all the grassroots energy and innovation. Perhaps we are at the beginning of that recognition as more and more political leaders are showing interest in FBOs. We must learn how to make the connections between spirituality and politics.

There is enormous potential here—not just for a few exemplary programs but for a new vision of real social change. It's a strategy that goes beyond left and right, engages the grassroots, and, best of all, might really work.

21

Our Hidden Safety Net

RAM CNAAN AND GAYNOR I. YANCEY

FROM COLONIAL TIMES, religious congregations and religious organizations in the United States have been providing not only for the spiritual needs of their congregants and communities but for their social welfare as well. Indeed, until the close of the nineteenth century, religious groups were virtually the nation's sole provider of social services. Social work, the profession now dedicated to caring for the human and social needs of society's most disadvantaged members, is rooted in religious theology and practice but is now distanced from faith-based social services.

The split between faith-based social services and social work began at the turn of the twentieth century. In 1897 Reverend Samuel H. Gurteen organized the Buffalo Charity Organization Society, modeled on similar groups in London and Glasgow whose new philosophy was that the needs of the poor should be met not only by members of religious congregations but also by the wealthy of the community at large. Under the influence of these societies, social services gradually traded their community-religious base for one that was citywide, temporal, and professional. The delivery of social services became less arbitrary and more systematic, and social work became increasingly secular, in a process that reached its culmination in 1935 with the enactment of the Social Security Act.

But despite the secular evolution of the welfare state, religious congregations have quietly continued to provide social services over the years. And as the nation's social needs have become more urgent over the past few decades, religious congregations have responded. They may well be providing more social services than ever before. I use the phrase "may well be" advisedly. Little hard data exist on the extent of social service provision by congregations now or in earlier times.

In this article I report the findings of my 1997 study, supported by Partners for Sacred Places, of 113 historic churches—all built before 1940 and still used as places of worship—in six American cities. Its purpose is to document the extent to which religious congregations are involved in community social service activity.

What Services?

My study consisted of extensive interviews by a research team with clergy, lay leaders, and social service providers in mostly urban churches in Chicago, Indianapolis, Mobile, New York, Philadelphia, and San Francisco. Congregation size ranged widely, from a low of 20 to a high of 4,800, with an average membership of 624. Most congregations consisted mostly of one ethnic group. Of the 113 congregations, 90 reported that three-quarters or more of their members belonged to one ethnic group, usually either African American or Caucasian. The congregations ranged from politically and theologically conservative (the former tended to cluster in Indianapolis and Mobile, the latter in Indianapolis, Mobile, and Philadelphia) to politically and theologically liberal (the former in San Francisco, Chicago, New York, and Philadelphia, the latter in San Francisco, Chicago, and New York). Though some denominations were overrepresented in particular cities, overall the sampling of denominational distribution was reasonably well balanced: 9 Presbyterian, 18 Baptist, 22 Episcopal, 11 Methodist, 18 Catholic, 10 Lutheran, and 25 others, including Jewish synagogues, independent churches, Pentecostal churches, and Friends Societies.

The 113 congregations in the sample reported providing a total of 449 social programs. One hundred and two (91 percent) provided at least one social service, and most offered more. Ninety-three percent of congregations in New York and 81 percent of those in Chicago reported offering five or more programs, as did 56 percent in Indianapolis, 50 percent in San Francisco, 44 percent in Philadelphia, and 24 percent in Mobile (the low number of social programs in Mobile may be attributable to the more rural character of the congregations studied). The social services varied widely, an indication that congregations were targeting the unique needs of their communities. Programs offered most frequently included food pantries (almost 60 percent of the congregations), music performances (56 percent), clothing closets (52 percent), holiday celebrations (52 percent), community bazaars and fairs (50 percent), choral groups (50 percent), international relief (50 percent), recreational programs for teens (45 percent), alliances with neighborhood associations (44 percent), visits to patients in hospitals (44 percent), visits to the sick (43 percent), soup kitchens (41 percent), and recreational programs for children (41 percent).

Each of the six cities in the study tended to have a distinct profile. Chicago and Indianapolis congregations, for example, were especially involved in providing permanent housing for needy people; community economic development; and programs for families, for children and youth, for homeless and poor people, and for other people in need. Mobile congregations provided many programs for children and youth, services for homeless and poor people, and programs for permanent housing, but they were less involved in assisting refugees, immigrants, or prisoners. New York congregations were quite distinct, specializing in arts and culture and in community organizing, such as boycotts and protests. They offered few programs for children and few for refugees, immigrants, or prisoners. Philadelphia congregations offered more programs for seniors, children, and youth, as well as educational opportunities for adults. They were less involved in services for the homeless and poor people or for refugees, immigrants, or prisoners. San Francisco congregations offered many programs for homeless and poor people, services for poor immigrants and refugees, health programs, and community security services. They offered fewer programs for families, seniors, or children.

Who Participates?

Who benefits from the social services these religious congregations provide? Congregation members take part in the programs' services, of course, but they are far outnumbered by nonmembers. For the total sample, the mean number of participants per program provided by or housed in a local religious congregation was 207. The mean number of congregation members was 40—a ratio of nonmembers to members of 4.2 to 1. Broken down by city, the ratio of nonmembers to members was 3.2 to 1 in Chicago; 7.1 to 1 in Indianapolis; 1.9 to 1 in Mobile; 2.9 to 1 in New York; 5.2 to 1 in Philadelphia; and 6.3 to 1 in San Francisco. Clearly, the many social and community programs offered by local religious congregations are designed to benefit the community at large.

Although some services, such as Alcoholics Anonymous or Boy Scouts, were provided in the congregation's quarters entirely by nonmembers, members often assisted community volunteers. For the total sample, members slightly outnumbered nonmembers in providing services—by a ratio of 1.1 to 1. In Chicago and Indianapolis, nonmembers providing services slightly outnumbered members, indicating that the congregations were more likely to be involved in joint efforts with the community rather than in direct service to their community. In New York, Philadelphia, and San Francisco, by contrast, members providing services outnumbered nonmembers by roughly 2 to 1; the ratio was almost 3 to 1 in Mobile.

The Financial Commitment

How much did their social programs cost the congregations? Of 240 reported programs involving monetary expenditures by the congregations, 7 were unusually costly (more than $5,000 a month). Those we omitted from our calculations so as not to bias our findings upward. Of 233 remaining programs with monetary costs, the mean monthly cost was $691. Monthly costs were highest in New York ($1,006), lowest in Indianapolis ($558). In addition to direct monetary support, congregations also provided space, particularly parish and fellowship halls and kitchens, classrooms, basements, and sanctuaries. The average market value of the space provided for each program was $562 per month.

The value of church volunteers' time was also considerable. Of the 449 programs in the entire sample, 338 used volunteers. The monthly number of volunteer hours for the whole sample of congregations was 49,892, which averages out to 148 hours per program per month. Indianapolis reported the highest mean, 220 hours; Philadelphia reported the lowest, 79 hours. In 1991 the Independent Sector, a national organization studying volunteer activity nationwide, assessed the value of a volunteer hour at $11.58. Using that figure results in an estimated monthly value for the whole sample of $577,751. Clergy and staff also invest considerable time in community service programs. For the sample as a whole, clergy were involved in 236 of the 449 programs and staff in 216 programs. Clergy averaged 19 hours of work per program per month; staff averaged 67 hours.

Congregations also provided valuable in-kind support and utilities. In-kind support such as the use of phones, printing, photocopying, and postage, was reported for 191 of the 449 programs at a mean cost of $71 per month. The cost of utilities—heating the building, cleaning it, wear-and-tear—amounted to a mean of $218 a month for the 182 programs reporting such costs.

When we added the total costs reported for the programs and divided the result by the total number of programs, including nonreporting programs, we found that the average monetary value of a program was $3,177 a month—or $38,124 a year. Broken down by city, the lowest average monthly cost per program was in Philadelphia ($2,025); the highest cost was in Indianapolis ($4,157).

For the entire sample, the mean share of the annual operating budget allocated to social ministry was 17.4 percent. The highest share was 21.2 percent (in Philadelphia); the lowest was 13.1 percent (in Mobile).

Any money income or in-kind services received by the congregations in return for their support was minimal. Few programs generated any income for the congregations. Of the 54 that did, the mean was $771 per program per month, or $93 averaged out over the entire sample. Another 50 programs reported in-kind support valued at a mean of $903 per reporting program, or $101 per program for the whole sample.

The net congregational contribution to society (the total monthly per program contribution—$3,177—less the monthly per program income, $194) was $2,984 per program per month, or $35,803 per program per year. On average, the subsidy congregations gave to their community programs was valued at more than $140,000 a year. Note, however, that this mean is the value of the program, not the actual fiscal cost accrued by the studied congregations. In other words, we measured the value of services if they were given as a volunteer labor or as part of the maintenance of the congregation, as an equivalent secular service will require such services to be paid for with real money

How Congregations Get Involved

The people most influential in initiating social services in our sample were the clergy and individual members or groups in the congregations. Congregational committees and staff members also initiated services. Few programs were organized in response to requests from people or groups outside the congregation. Together, other congregations, diocese, judicatory, neighborhood coalitions, human service organizations, and government agencies were responsible for initiating just over 15 percent of all reported social programs.

Many of the programs—165 of the total of 449—were begun in response to a change in the community. Of the others, 63 grew out of local cutbacks in public spending, 61 out of cuts in state spending, and 67 out of cuts in federal spending. New York reported the greatest response to cuts in public spending. Such cuts spurred few social programs in Indianapolis and Mobile. There, congregations reported that community service was a way to witness their faith. In fact, congregations did not see government cutbacks as the reason for their involvement. Rather, they told us that they reacted to observed needs in the community

A Beacon in the Night

In an era in which mutual aid societies are practically vanishing, religious congregations continue to carry out social programs in most American communities. Their perseverance in an era of downsizing and declining corporate support is a clear message to their neighbors and society at large of resolution and faith. A 1995 study by Sidney Verba, Kay Lehman

Scholzman, and Henry E. Brady found local religious congregations to be the most important source of civic competence in contemporary America, especially for people of low income.[1] Our findings support the importance of local religious congregations in enhancing local quality of life and contributing to the formation of civil society.

Today, as responsibility for social programs is being devolved from the federal government to state and local authorities, congregations and religiously affiliated entities—the least studied and least understood actors in contemporary public life—are beginning to gain notice in public discourse.

Not that the issue is simple. Some of the religious groups that provide social services adhere to values that are not popular and that can be offensive to some groups. Some Americans are uncomfortable with the notion that religious congregations consider providing social services to be ministry and yet are a key element of the local welfare system, actively supporting the neediest members of our society.

Congregations are highly involved in social service in their communities and beyond. Their voluntary effort serves as a vital backbone for civic society in America. That congregations throughout the nation come to the help of those in need is a uniquely American social institution, one that is insufficiently acknowledged publicly, let alone celebrated by the members of the congregations and their clergy.

Yet no matter how much congregations exert themselves, they cannot even begin to fill the gaps created by the devolution of federal responsibility for social welfare to states and localities. The impressive network of services provided by congregations is at best important locally, a complement to state services. And as important as providing social and community services is to religious congregations, it is nevertheless a secondary goal—and one dependent on the congregation's ability to master sufficient resources and human capital to reach it.

22

Religion and Public Life

JAMES Q. WILSON

RELIGION MAKES a large difference in the lives of millions of Americans despite the fact that American government is indifferent to it and hostile to its support. This may only appear to be a paradox. In fact, religion may be important in the United States in part because governmental indifference allows so many religions to prosper. Voltaire foresaw as much when he observed that a nation with one religion has oppression, a nation with two has civil war, and a nation with a hundred has peace. Much the same argument was made by Adam Smith.

Though the United States is a nation inhabited by people from other countries where religious observance is less important than it is here, the law and culture that sustain multiple sects have worked their effect on many who have arrived here, giving them a chance to form and organize around their own beliefs, to create and sustain their own churches, and to proclaim and defend their own visions. America enjoys religious freedom, and accordingly many religions have prospered. Freedom of religious expression has not stunted religion, it has encouraged it.

It has especially encouraged the kind of religion that is often called fundamentalist. Churches that, by their own beliefs, feel it necessary to reach out and organize others—churches, that is, in which the missionary impulse is particularly strong—are the ones that most benefit from religious freedom. Missionary churches depend for their survival on the people whom they can convert, and so they are the ones most likely to reflect the wants and needs of ordinary people. More traditional churches, with little missionary impulse, are at a disadvantage. They will often find their numbers dwindling because they have no serious impulse to increase these numbers. Put simplistically, a traditional church is one to which its nominal members repair when getting married or buried but to which they rarely give their regular attention. A fundamentalist church, by contrast, is one that can exist only if it succeeds in drawing to it people for whom religion makes a daily difference.

Fundamentalist churches not only benefit from religious liberty, they contribute to it. David Hume explained why. Those religions that rely on what he called "enthusiasm," that is, on a belief in direct and divine illumination—lead to more furious passions but in time to greater civil liberty. The reason, Hume observed in his essay "On Superstition and Enthusiasm," is that enthusiasm is both the enemy of hierarchical churches and an expression of animated people who cherish liberty. What we now call a fundamentalist church—one that believes that people can acquire a direct knowledge of God without priestly intervention—depends on the religious equivalent of the entrepreneurial spirit, just as a small business person, unlike the politically more powerful large corporation, depends on economic freedom.

For these reasons, and for others I do not yet understand, religious observance is more common in the United States than in many other industrialized nations, even though this country was settled by people from the very nations where such observances are less customary.

This great force in American life makes a difference in human life. This is a matter to which scholars have given relatively little attention because scholars, especially in the humanities and the social sciences, are disproportionately drawn from the ranks of people who are indifferent—or even hostile—to religion. But if a creed did not make some difference, far fewer people would embrace it.

Religion and Morality

Religion affects morality, but not in the way many people suppose. Let me repeat here an argument made more fully by Michael Oakeshott in *Reli-*

gion, Politics, and the Moral Life.[1] Religion, I think, can neither be the source
of morality nor provide the support for morality. It cannot be the source
because it is obvious that there are highly moral people who are not religious and fanatical extremists who are deeply religious. In every nation
there are many moral people who have few or weak religious views and act
morally without reference to a religious doctrine. Occasionally, an entire
nation seems unreligiously moral. Japan is often held up, rightly, as a nation remarkably free of the worse excesses of crime, drug abuse, and political violence, yet Japan has achieved this record, one that cannot be duplicated
by any other advanced industrial nation, without much that resembles religious commitment. Religion is rarely, even in its sermons and writings, a
true source of morality. When Jesus told us of the Golden Rule, he was not
telling us anything we had not known before; he was only reminding us
that, though we knew this rule, we were often violating it. As Samuel Johnson
was later to put it, people need to be reminded more often that they need
to be instructed.

Nor is it the case that religion provides the main sanction for a moral
code. Many people believe that the natural life of humans cannot supply a
guide to human action. If we think that by contemplating who we are and
how society is organized we can find a principle of right conduct, we commit what some have called the naturalistic fallacy. This problem leads many
to believe that human nature is so devoid of moral sentiments that any
moral code of action must require divine revelation. We are then induced
to obey that code either out of a desire to please the God that supplied it or
out of a desire to avoid the threat of eternal damnation or to acquire
otherworldly pleasures.

The desire to please God is a worthy one, but it is not clear that pleas-
ing the commands of a superior force is sufficient to define an act as moral.
It would be equivalent to acting morally because we wish to please a friend.
That is not an unworthy motive and is indeed the source of much moral
behavior, but it does raise a question: does moral action require subordina-
tion to another party? Perhaps to some extent, but not to every extent.
Morality entirely defined as obedience to a superior being becomes identi-
cal to blind obedience. It suggests that morality depends on obedience even
though many people make moral choices without such obedience. They
make those choices because the so-called naturalistic fallacy is itself a fal-

lacy: there are aspects of human nature and of the social order that generate moral sentiments.

A clearer argument against the view that religion enforces morality arises when we consider people who follow a rule to avoid threats or acquire pleasures. Can we be called moral if we avoid stealing only when a police officer is watching or contribute to charity only when we are applauded at a banquet? I think not.

Religion's chief contribution to morality is to enable people to transform their lives. This is not an easy process and requires of people an act of faith that many persons cannot supply and few will sustain. A profound act of faith does not necessarily make us better, it only makes us more knowledgeable. We come to know God and through Him to know ourselves. And what we learn about ourselves is, I suspect, quite unsettling. We are weak, greedy, impassioned, ill-tempered, and contradictory; we can barely be good any of the time, much less most of the time. As Christopher Lasch put it in *The Revolt of the Elites and the Betrayal of Democracy*, religion, far from putting doubts and anxieties to rest, tends to intensify them.[2]

The people for whom a religious experience heightens doubts and sharpens anxieties are people who are leading wasted or immoral lives. Religion does not solve their problems; it heightens them to the point that people finally feel they ought to do something about them. It creates an opportunity for personal transformation.

Consider the single most important organized example of personal transformation we have. It was created by neither churches nor businesses nor government, but by a few people whose lives had become unlivable. It is called Alcoholics Anonymous. Started in 1935, it does not impart a religion but uses faith in a supreme being as a motivation for transforming the lives of drunkards. We are not quite certain why it works so well. We have no data, in part because AA has no interest in generating data (and a good thing, too). But whatever makes it work for many (but far from all) of its members, it signifies the importance of self-discovery and personal transformation in human life.

Despite the general indifference of social science to religion, we can clutch at other bits of evidence. Several studies have found that, other things being equal, those who are religious are less likely to be criminal than those who are irreligious.[3] There is even some sketchy evidence that faith-based

prison programs are more likely to improve the lives of inmates after they
are released than are rehabilitative programs that do not involve religion.
And in every big city and many small cities in America, church-based groups
are working at reducing delinquency, drug abuse, gang wars, teenage pregnancy, and single-parent homes. We have no systematic evidence as to
whether these programs are working in any large sense—that is, for lots of
people—but ample testimony that they do work in a small sense—that is,
by changing the lives of identifiable individuals.

Government and Religion

The evidence, though not conclusive, does suggest rather strongly that religion can make a difference in the lives of people about whom we worry,
and ought to worry, the most. Can the government take advantage of the
transforming power of religion without corrupting its use through heavy-
handed regulations and endless litigation? To answer that question, we must
acknowledge the great importance of the First Amendment to the Constitution and then deplore the sorry state of law that has emerged about its
implications.

The second part of that amendment is the "free exercise" clause that
denies the federal government the power to prohibit or require religious
practices. It guarantees, in short, freedom of religious conscience. Not only
does that rule keep the government's hands out of our religious—or irreligious—beliefs, it also facilitates the growth of religion by permitting new
faiths and churches to spring up as people respond to them. Enforcing the
free exercise clause offers some problems, in particular that of regulating
behavior that may have a religious motivation. The courts have said we are
free to believe but not necessarily free to act. Thus the courts will not always permit what a religion commends. In consequence, they have allowed
the government to ban Mormon polygamy and have not allowed the Amish
to exempt themselves from paying Social Security taxes; they have upheld a
ban on Indian use of peyote for religious reasons but have allowed religiously justified animal sacrifice.

Though the free exercise clause is a fount of continual litigation, its
general purpose remains clear. It was well understood when first put into
the Bill of Rights: no one, so far as anyone can tell, disagreed with the view

that everyone should have religious freedom to worship or not as each saw fit. Nothing of the sort can be said about the preceding part of the amendment, the so-called establishment clause. No one, including whoever wrote it, has ever provided a clear understanding of it. James Madison proposed to the first Congress language specifying that no "national religion" shall be established. Once it got to the floor of the House, it was changed to read "Congress shall make no law establishing religion." In the Senate, the language was still different: "Congress shall make no law establishing articles of faith, or a mode of worship." Though different, all these versions had two things in common: they were restrictions on what the federal government, not state governments, could do, and they were aimed at preventing Congress from creating a church or telling people how to worship in one. What emerged from the conference committee was the ambiguous language we now have: "Congress shall make no law respecting an establishment of religion."

What in the world does "respecting" mean? No one has any idea. The members of Congress who voted for it left no commentary, nor did anyone else. The Supreme Court, however, has created its own commentary. The decisive case, *Everson* v. *Board of Education* of Ewing Township, was decided in 1947. In it, the Court allowed New Jersey to reimburse parents for bus fare to school, including to parochial schools. But in the same ruling, it announced that the "respecting" clause erected a "wall of separation" between church and state. That phrase was written by Thomas Jefferson in 1802 in a letter to a group of Baptists in Danbury, Connecticut. Jefferson, recall, was not at the constitutional convention and was not a member of the Congress that wrote the First Amendment. He was in no position at all to explain what "respecting" meant. Moreover, he was a religious radical who had worked hard to separate church and state in ways that most politicians disliked. But the Supreme Court liked his phrase and decided that is what the clause meant.

Incoherent Case Law

Today it requires a lengthy textbook to describe the ways in which the Court has enforced the wall or permitted (as it did in the 1947 case) governments to dig under, crawl over, or run around the so-called wall. Consider how often the wall is breached: "In God We Trust" is printed on our dollar bills and "One nation, under God" is part of the Pledge of Allegiance, but we cannot permit a nativity scene to appear in a court house. The House and the Senate begin each meeting with a prayer, and the government pays ministers of various faiths to be chaplains for the armed services, but we cannot allow a nonsectarian prayer to begin a high school graduation. The federal government can use the G.I. bill to pay the tuition costs of veterans attending religious as well as sectarian colleges, but states cannot supply financial aid to students attending parochial schools.

It is pointless to belabor the obvious: the Supreme Court has created case law about the establishment clause that is to some significant degree incoherent. Incoherent, but not uncodified. In 1972, the Court, in the case of *Lemon* v. *Kurtzman,* set forth three rules for deciding when a statute could involve religion. First, the statute must have a secular purpose; second, its primary effect must be one that neither advances nor inhibits religion; and third, it must not foster an excessive entanglement with religion. But as Professor Henry Abraham has noted, on the very day that *Lemon* was announced, the Court decided that it was constitutional for the federal government to spend a quarter of a billion dollars for constructing buildings on private, including religious, college campuses. Among the reasons given by the author of this opinion, Chief Justice William Burger, was his claim that parochial colleges are less involved in religious indoctrination than are parochial high schools. May I enter a mild dissent? I attended a relentlessly Baptist college where chapel was compulsory and I (a Catholic student) was given as my academic adviser a Baptist professor who asked me why I did not become a Protestant.

The case law that has tumbled forward since the 1947 *Everson* decision cannot be reconciled by any set of rules. In 1947 New Jersey could reimburse parents for the bus fare they spent sending their children to parochial schools, but in 1972 the Court struck down an Ohio plan to give $90-per-year tuition rebates to children attending parochial school. In 1980 the Court allowed New York to reimburse parochial schools for certain state-mandated expenses even though in 1977 it had overturned New York's effort to reimburse parochial schools for certain kinds of record-keeping. In 1992 the Court said that a rabbi could not give a nonsectarian invocation at a public school graduation but a year later allowed a student-led graduation prayer.

The central problem that the Supreme Court has never faced is this: the First Amendment clearly prevents the government from requiring or imposing religious practices (such as a mandatory school prayer or paying tax money to a specific religious institution), but there is no substantial evidence that the framers of the First Amendment ever meant for it to ban nondiscriminatory government aid to all religions generally. The *Lemon* test is an error, because it forbids any government aid that might advance religion generally or that might "entangle" the government in religion, no matter how nondiscriminatory the aid or the entanglement.

Unwanted Government Pressure

But there is another side to the problem of government aid to religious institutions. Federal money brings federal rules, and federal rules can harm, distort, or even crush religious experiences and greatly burden the small ministries of most churches and synagogues. Getting and accounting for government money is a task for a trained lawyer and accountant; most churches lack the services of such professionals. Though Congress might have the sense to modify the regulations now governing institutions it funds, left unchecked one can imagine a church grant being subject to a minority group set-aside, church leadership being reshaped by equal employment opportunity criteria, and church membership falling under the Americans with Disabilities Act. Government aid tends to turn aid recipients into the organizational equivalent of the bureaucracy that supplies the aid. The essence of the religious experience is, I think, not one that could be supplied under the aegis of the Federal Register and the United States Code. Imagine what would have happened to Alcoholics Anonymous if it had taken federal money. Its mission would have been shaped by government advisers and its appropriation defended by an AA pressure group.

I suspect many, probably most, Americans want to have the government—though not necessarily government aid—held at arm's length from religious institutions. Though there seems to be widespread support for allowing school prayer (a mistake, in my view), there is also widespread aversion to making religious activity mandatory. Americans are, more than the people of almost any other industrialized nation, religious, but as Alan Wolfe has pointed out in his new book *One Nation After All*, Americans are reluctant to impose religious views on other people.[4] His data suggest to me that though Americans are opposed to a constitutional wall of separation between church and state, they tend to support a cultural wall. That cultural wall seems to reflect the growing American recognition that we are, indeed, a multicultural society in which every group owes every other one a substantial degree of respect. Wolfe suggests that Americans are loyal to "the essential truths of transcendental moral principles," but they are also willing to apply them flexibly. By flexibly, Wolfe means with reasonable deference to the personal and cultural circumstances in which ordinary people find themselves.

What Is to Be Done?

If religion is an important source of possible personal transformation but any direct involvement between the government and religion will be denied by the Court, corrupted by Congress, and opposed by the public, what is to be done? I suggest that we must facilitate the movement of private funds into church-connected enterprises that have as their goal the kind of personal transformation that is required if we are to rescue people from social pathology.

A great deal of money—in 1993 as much as $57 billion—now goes from individual Americans to religious groups. Most of this money is to support churches and synagogues; not much, I suspect, is for important forms of religious outreach. And however the money is used, very little comes from corporations or foundations. Yet corporations contribute large amounts to secular establishments—schools, hospitals, and cultural entities.

We need a faith-based equivalent of the United Way. Not exactly the United Way, of course, but rather an independent organization that identifies useful faith-based outreach programs aimed at the kinds of personal misconduct—alcoholism, crime, delinquency, drug abuse, and single-mom pregnancies—about which Americans are so deeply, and so rightly, concerned. There are countless such church-based efforts. John DiIulio and his associates have catalogued them in several cities. We now need to move beyond a catalogue and toward a switchboard that will direct private giving toward useful programs.

By "useful" a scholar usually means "empirically tested," but empirical tests are hard to arrange for small, understaffed, and underfunded activities. It would be better to limit the word useful to mean having passed a few simple tests: the program is aimed at reaching people at risk for harmful behavior, is financially honest and intellectually serious, and has won the esteem of knowledgeable observers. In time, perhaps we shall know more about such efforts; some might even be evaluated. But initially, evaluation is much less important than effort.

The amount of money that could be raised by a United Way for Religious Outreach is not trivial. Corporations almost never give their charitable dollars to religious groups, in part because they believe, rightly, that supporting churches is a task for church members and in part because they fear, understandably, criticism from people skeptical of religious activity. But the employees of corporations can make contributions to a variety of enterprises in ways that lead to their donations being matched by corporate funds up to some annual limit. Rarely, however, are faith-based outreach programs on the list of charities approved for such matches. If in each large city there was a United Way for Religious Outreach, it could provide guidance for corporations willing to look for church-based outreach programs and for corporate employees eager to contribute to a particular kind of church outreach. Both corporations and individuals now give money to programs designed to help the needy, but only the largest ones attract support. The Salvation Army, for example, deservedly gets such support, but smaller versions of the same religious effort—small churches with one or two ministers and a handful of volunteers—get nothing.

Helping the kind of personal transformation that is the core function of religion requires that we expect no broad changes, little in the way of a mass movement, and not much in the form of verifiable data. Faith can only transform one person at a time, and then only as the result of the personal attention of one other person. This is not an activity of which research foundations or schools of public policy know much. Or care much. But it is, over the course of human history, a powerful force that has shaped nations and cultures. We ought not let constitutional scruples or personal reservations impede what may be the last best hope of the utterly disadvantaged.

Notes

Notes to E. J. Dionne Jr. and John J. DiIulio Jr.

1. Andrew Greeley, "The Other America, Religion and Social Capital," *American Prospect*, no. 32 (May–June 1997).

2. Glenn C. Loury, "Cast Out by the Right," *New York Times*, November 30, 1997, sec. D, p. 9.

3. Mark Chaves, "Religious Congregations and Welfare Reform: Who Will Take Advantage of Charitable Choice?" *American Sociological Review*, vol. 64 (December 1999), pp. 836–46.

4. Amy Sherman, *Restorers of Hope: Reaching the Poor in Your Community with Church-Based Ministries That Work* (Crossway Books, 1997).

5. Gabriel Fackre, ed., *Judgment Day at the White House: A Critical Declaration Exploring Moral Issues and the Political Use and Abuse of Religion* (Eerdmans, 1999).

6. Gregg Easterbrook, *Beside Still Waters: Searching for Meaning in an Age of Doubt* (William Morrow and Company, 1998).

Notes to W. Bradford Wilcox and John P. Bartkowski

1. James C. Dobson, "Newsletter from Dr. Dobson," *Focus on the Family*, July 1998 (http://www.family.org/docstudy/newsletters/a0002203.html [April 19, 2000]).

2. Patricia Ireland, "Beware of 'Feel-Good Male Supremacy' " *Washington Post,* September 7, 1997, p. C3.

3. Cokie Roberts and Steven V. Roberts, "Southern Baptists Have a Distorted View of the Family," *Denver Rocky Mountain News,* June 21, 1998, p. 3B.

4. Dobson, "Newsletter."

5. Melinda Lundquist and Christian Smith, "The Triumph of Ambivalence: American Evangelicals on Sex-Roles and Marital Decision-Making," paper presented at the annual meeting of the Society for the Scientific Study of Religion, 1998, Montreal.

6. Christopher G. Ellison, John P. Bartkowski, and Michelle L. Segal, "Conservative Protestantism and the Parental Use of Corporal Punishment," *Social Forces,* vol. 74 (1996), pp. 1003–29.

7. Ralph LaRossa, "Fatherhood and Social Change," *Family Relations,* vol. 37 (1988), pp. 451–57, esp. p. 451.

8. Duane F. Alwin, "Religion and Parental Childrearing Orientations: Evidence of a Catholic-Protestant Convergence," *American Journal of Sociology,* vol. 92 (1986), pp. 412–40.

9. James Davison Hunter, *Evangelicalism: The Coming Generation* (University of Chicago Press, 1997), p. 79.

10. Christian Smith, *American Evangelicalism: Embattled and Thriving* (University of Chicago Press, 1998).

Notes to Richard Parker

1. Karl Marx, "On the Jewish Question," in Karl Marx and Friedrich Engels, *Collected Works,* v. III (London: Lawrence and Wisehart), p. 151. Emphasis in original.

2. Cf. Meredith Ramsay, "Rebuilding the Cities," *Urban Affairs Review* (May 1998), p. 611.

3. Gary Wills, *Under God: Religion and American Politics* (Simon and Schuster, 1990), pp. 15–16.

4. George Gallup Jr. and D. Michael Lindsay, *Surveying the Religious Landscape* (Morehouse, 1999).

5. Wills, *Under God.*

6. On percentage of religious Americans, see Gallup Jr. and Lindsay, *Surveying the Religious Landscape.*

7. The 1,200 figure is in the *Yearbook of American and Canadian Churches* (Nashville, Tenn.: Abingdon Press, 1998).

8. Kenneth Wald, *Religion and Politics in the United States*, 3d ed. (Washington: Congressional Quarterly, 1997), p. 185 (abortion) and p. 207 (school funding).

9. "Social Principles," *The Book of Resolutions of the United Methodist Church* (Nashville: Abingdon Press, 1992), p. 44.

10. Membership numbers for the Methodists and other denominations cited are from Gallup and Lindsay, *Surveying the Religious Landscape.*

11. Thad Williamson, "True Prophecy? A Critical Examination of the Sociopolitical Stance of the Mainline Protestant Churches," *Union Seminary Quarterly Review*, vol. 51 (1997), pp. 79–116.

12. Cf. "Eradicating Poverty and Improving the Human Habitat" and "Theological Ethics and Political Participation," both in *Church and Society* 87:1 (1996), pp. 95–97 and 55–58.

13. Robert Lichter and others, *The Media Elite* (Adler and Adler, 1986), cited in Dart and Allen, *Bridging the Gap: Religion and the News Media* (Nashville, Tenn.: Freedom Forum First Amendment Center, no date), p. 42.

14. H. Richard Niebuhr, *Social Sources of Denominationalism* (Henry Holt, 1929).

15. Cf. Sydney Ahlstrom, *A Religious History of the American People* (Yale University Press, 1972), p. 1079.

16. Robert Wuthnow, "Mobilizing for Civic Engagement," unpublished, Princeton University.

17. "One in ten" data from studies cited in Wald, *Religion and Politics in the United States*, p. 245. "Gallup" is from George Gallup Jr. and Sarah Jones, *100 Questions and Answers: Religion in America* (Princeton, N.J.: Princeton Religion Research Center), p. 142.

18. Cf. David Shribman, "Frustrated Christian Right Tests Its Faith in Politics," *Boston Globe*, July 5, 1999, p. 1.

Notes to Alan Wolfe

1. The declaration can be found in Gabriel Fackre, ed., *Judgment Day at the White House: A Critical Declaration Exploring Moral Issues and the Political Use and Abuse of Religion* (Eerdmans, 1999), quotation on p. 1.

2. Ibid., p. 14.

3. Ibid.

4. Ibid., p. 114.

5. Ibid., p. 28.

6. Ibid., p. 18.

7. Ibid., p. 15.

8. Michael Walzer, *The Company of Critics: Social Criticism and Political Commitment in the Twentieth Century* (Basic Books, 1988).

Notes to E. J. Dionne Jr.

1. Nathan Glazer, "Fundamentalism: A Defensive Offensive," in Richard John Neuhaus and Michael Cromartie, eds., *Piety and Politics: Evangelicals and Fundamentalists Confront the World* (Washington: Ethics and Public Policy Center, 1987), pp. 250–51.

2. Richard John Neuhaus, *The Naked Public Square: Religion and Democracy in America* (Eerdmans, 1984).

3. Stephen L. Carter, *The Culture of Disbelief: How American Law and Politics Trivialize Religious Devotion* (Doubleday and Company, 1994).

Notes to John J. DiIulio Jr.

1. George Gallup Jr., "Religion in America: Will the Vitality of Churches Be the Surprise of the Next Century?" *Public Perspective* (October-November 1995), p. 4.

2. W. E. B. Dubois, *The Philadelphia Negro: A Social Study* (University of Pennsylvania Press, 1996), p. 203.

3. Eric C. Lincoln and Lawrence H. Mamiya, *The Black Church in the African-American Experience* (Duke University Press, 1990), pp. 15, 151.

4. James Q. Wilson, "Two Nations," Francis Boyer lecture, American Enterprise Institute, Washington, December 1997, p. 10; David B. Larson and Byron R. Johnson, *Religion: The Forgotten Factor in Cutting Youth Crime and Saving At-Risk Youth* (Manhattan Institute, Center for Civic Innovation, 1998); and T. David Evans and others, "Religion and Crime Reexamined: The Impact of Religion, Secular Controls, and Social Ecology on Adult Criminality," *Criminology*, vol. 33 (1995), pp. 211–12.

5. Richard B. Freeman, "Who Escapes? The Relation of Church-Going and Other Background Factors to the Socio-Economic Performance of Black Male Youths from Inner-City Poverty Tracts," Working Paper 1656 (Cambridge, Mass.: National Bureau of Economic Research, 1985); Larson and Johnson, *Religion;* and

Byron R. Johnson and others, *The "Invisible Institution" and Black Youth Crime: The Church as an Agency of Local Social Control* (Philadelphia: Center for Research on Relgion and Urban Civil Society, forthcoming), p. 21.

6. Cynthia Sipe and Patricia Ma, *Support for Youth: A Profile of Three Communities* (Philadelphia, Pa.: Public/Private Ventures, 1998).

7. Interview with Gary Walker by author, June 1998.

8. Andrew Billingsley "The Social Relevance of the Contemporary Black Church," *National Journal of Sociology*, vol. 8 (Summer-Winter 1994).

9. Interview with Harold Dean Trulear by author, June 1998.

10. Robert L. Woodson Sr., *The Triumphs of Joseph: How Today's Community Healers Are Reviving Our Streets and Neighborhoods* (Free Press, 1998).

Note to Ronald J. Sider and Heidi Rolland Unruh

1. Stephen Monsma, *When Sacred and Secular Mix* (Lanham, Md.: Rowman and Littlefield, 1996), p. 68.

Notes to Melissa Rogers

1. *Hunt* v. *McNair*, 413 U.S. 734, 743 (1973).

2. *Bowen* v. *Kendrick*, 487 U.S. 589, 610 (1988) (quoting *Grand Rapids School District* v. *Ball*, 473 U.S. 373, 385 [1985]).

3. M. B. Taboada, "Gov. Bush Visits City for Bill-Signing," *Dallas Morning News*, June 13, 1997, p. 1A.

4. George W. Bush for President website (http://www.georgewbush.com/issues/domestic/faith/barriers.asp, Issues—Faith-Based Initiatives).

5. Al Gore for President website (http://www.algore2000.com/speeches/speeches_faith_052499.html, remarks as prepared for delivery by Vice President Al Gore on the Role of Faith-Based Organizations, May 24, 1999, Atlanta).

6. The Personal Responsibility and Work Opportunity Reconciliation Act of 1996, 42 U.S.C. § 604a(j) (Supp. 1999).

7. Al Gore for President website.

8. Ibid.

9. The Personal Responsibility and Work Opportunity Reconciliation Act of 1996.

10. *Congressional Record*, November 10, 1999, Debate on Fathers Count Act of 1999 (H.R. 3073) (http://www.thomas.loc.gov/home/thomas.html).

11. *Dodge* v. *Salvation Army*, 1989 U.S. Dist. LEXIS 4797 (S.D. Miss. 1989).

12. *Pedreira* v. *Kentucky Baptist Homes for Children,* Civ. Action No. 3: OOCV-210-S, filed April 17, 2000 (W. D. Ky).

13. Al Gore for President website.

Notes to Jim Wallis

1. Vice President Al Gore, "The Role of Faith-Based Organizations," May 24, 1999, Atlanta, Ga.

2. Governor George W. Bush, "The Duty of Hope," July 22, 1999, Indianapolis, Ind.

3. Reverend Eugene Rivers, speech to Call to Renewal National Summit, January 31, 1999.

4. Personal correspondence with author.

Note to Ram Cnaan and Gaynor I. Yancey

1. Sidney Verba, Kay Lehman Schlozman, and Henry E. Brady, *Voice and Equality: Civic Voluntarism in American Politics* (Harvard University Press, 1995).

Notes to James Q. Wilson

1. Michael Oakeshott, "Religion and the Moral Life," in Timothy Fuller, ed., *Religion, Politics, and the Moral Life* (Yale University Press, 1993), pp. 39–45.

2. Christopher Lasch, *The Revolt of the Elites and the Betrayal of Democracy* (W. W. Norton, 1996), pp. 14–16.

3. T. David Evans and others, "Religion and Crime Reexamined," *Criminology*, vol. 33 (1995), pp. 195–224.

4. Alan Wolfe, *One Nation After All* (Viking, 1997).

Contributors

John P. Bartkowski is assistant professor of sociology at Mississippi State University. He and W. Bradford Wilcox are studying parental and marital behavior among American Evangelicals. Their essay is adapted from an article that appeared in the Summer 1999 issue of the *Responsive Community* (Summer 1990), reprinted with permission.

Robert J. Blendon, of Harvard's Kennedy School of Government and the Harvard School of Public Health; **John M. Benson**, of the Harvard School of Public Health; **Mollyann Brodie, Drew E. Altman**, and **Nina Kjellson**, of the Henry J. Kaiser Family Foundation; and **Claudia Deane** and **Richard Morin** of the *Washington Post* are part of a team conducting ongoing polling on Americans' knowledge, belief, and attitudes about domestic policy.

Taylor Branch is author of *Parting the Waters* (Simon and Schuster, 1988) and *Pillar of Fire* (Simon and Schuster, 1999). His article is from *Parting the Waters* by Taylor Branch. Copyright © 1988 by Taylor Branch. Published by Touchstone, $16.00. Reprinted by permission of Simon and Schuster.

Tony Campolo is a professor at Eastern College. A well-known evangelical leader, he was selected by President Bill Clinton as one of the president's spiritual counselors in the wake of the Monica Lewinsky scandal.

Ram Cnaan is an associate professor in the University of Pennsylvania School of Social Work. He is the author of *Social and Community Involvement of Religious Congregations Housed in Historic Religious Properties*, a report commissioned by Partners for Sacred Places. The article by Cnaan and Yancey is drawn from that report.

John J. Dilulio Jr. is Frederick Fox Leadership Professor of Politics, Religion, and Civil Society and Professor of Political Science, University of Pennsylvania; nonresident senior fellow at Brookings; and senior fellow, Manhattan Institute.

E. J. Dionne is a senior fellow in Governmental Studies at Brookings and a columnist for the *Washington Post*. His article originally appeared in the *Washington Post* on October 3, 1999, reprinted with permission. He is the author of *Why Americans Hate Politics* (Simon and Schuster, 1991) and *They Only Look Dead* (Simon and Schuster, 1996).

Ed Dobson, formerly with the Moral Majority, serves as pastor of Calvary Church in Grand Rapids, Michigan.

Jean Bethke Elshtain, author of *Who Are We? Critical Reflections; Hopeful Possibilities* (Eerdmans, 2000) is the Laura Spelman Rockefeller Professor of Social and Political Ethics, University of Chicago.

Patrick Glynn, associate director of the George Washington University Institute for Communitarian Policy Studies, is the author of *God:The Evidence* (Prima/Forum, 1997).

Stephen Goldsmith is the former Republican mayor of Indianapolis and is now a policy adviser to George W. Bush's presidential campaign.

Glenn Loury is University Professor, professor of economics, and director of the Institute on Race and Social Division at Boston University.

Richard N. Ostling is religion writer for the Associated Press. This article is drawn from a lecture at a 1999 symposium, *"K-12 Education: Perspectives on the Future,"* sponsored by the Van Andel Education Institute, Grand Rapids, Michigan.

Richard Parker is senior fellow at the Shorenstein Center on Press, Politics, and Public Policy, Kennedy School of Government, Harvard University. His article, in a different form, appeared in the *American Prospect*, vol. 11 (January 2000), reprinted with permission.

Melissa Rogers is general counsel at the Baptist Joint Committee on Public Affairs. Her article was adapted from "The Wrong Way to Do Right: Charitable Choice and Churches," in Derek Davis and Barry Hankins, eds., *Welfare Reform and Faith-Based Organizations* (Baylor University, J. M. Dawson Institute of Church-State Studies, 1999).

Kurt L. Schmoke is the former Democratic Mayor of Baltimore and is now at the law firm of Wilmer, Cutler and Pickering.

Ronald Sider, author of *Rich Christians in an Age of Hunger* (Word Books, 1997), is president of Evangelicals for Social Action.

Staci Simmons is associate director of the Pew Forum on Religion and Public Life.

Max L. Stackhouse is Stephen Colwell Professor of Christian Ethics and director of the Project on Public Theology at Princeton Theological Seminary.

Cal Thomas, former vice president for communications of the Moral Majority, is a syndicated columnist.

Heidi Rolland Unruh is a project analyst with Evangelicals for Social Action. Her article with Ronald Sider is drawn from "An (Ana)baptist Theological Perspective on Church-State Cooperation," in Derek Davis and Barry Hankins, eds., *Welfare Reform and Faith-Based Organizations* (Baylor University, J.M. Dawson Institute of Church-State Studies, 1999).

Jim Wallis is editor-in-chief of *Sojourners Magazine,* and convener of Call to Renewal, a national federation of churches and faith-based organizations working to overcome poverty. He is the author, most recently, of *Faith Works* (Random House, 2000).

Peter Wehner is executive director for policy, Empower America.

W. Bradford Wilcox is a doctoral student in cultural sociology at Princeton University and was a 1999 *Civitas* fellow at the Brookings Institution. He and John P. Bartkowski are studying parental and marital behavior among American Evangelicals. Their essay is adapted from an article that appeared in the Summer 1999 issue of the *Responsive Community* (Summer 1999), reprinted with permission.

James Q. Wilson is emeritus professor of management and public policy at the University of California at Los Angeles and the author, most recently, of *The Moral Sense* (Free Press, 1993).

Alan Wolfe, the author of *One Nation After All* (Penguin, 1999), is professor of political science and director of the Center for Religion and American Public Life at Boston College.

Gaynor I. Yancey is assistant professor at Baylor University School of Social Work. She was the research director for the report commissioned by *Partners for Sacred Places.*

Index